Cézanne
DRAWINGS

Alfred Neumeyer

DRAWINGS

A BITTNER ART BOOK

NEW YORK   THOMAS YOSELOFF   *LONDON*

The name of owners refers only to those not yet listed in Venturi's *Catalogue Raisonné* (1936). The same applies to bibliographical references.

Measurements different from Venturi's listings are based on new checking.

Dates differing from Venturi are explained in the catalogue text.

THOMAS YOSELOFF, PUBLISHER

11 East 36th Street

New York 16, N. Y.

THOMAS YOSELOFF LTD.

123 New Bond Street

London W. 1, England

TO
MY WIFE

PREFACE

I ACKNOWLEDGE GRATEFULLY THE GENEROUS SUPPORT which I have received in the preparation of this volume by my colleagues of the print and drawing cabinets of museums here and abroad. Collectors and dealers listed in the catalogue section have provided me with photographs and information, and only through their cooperation has this volume been made possible.

Whoever produces a work on Cézanne owes, of course, tribute to Lionello Venturi, whose *Catalogue Raisonné* remains the basis of all research. John Rewald's publications on this artist also belong to the solid substructure of any subsequent publication. Other books used to advantage by the author are listed in the bibliography. In my search for the material I have received the friendliest help from Mr. John Rewald and from Mons. André Chappuis, the author of two books on Cézanne drawings. My sincerest thanks go to Mrs. Ariel Parkinson who has revised this manuscript.

In the selection of drawings and watercolors it has been my aim to choose equally from the four subject matters into which I have grouped the material: nudes and figure studies, portraits, still lifes, and landscapes. Rather than mixing the four groups, I have tried to show the growth of Cézanne's art each time anew. It is hoped that in this manner the viewer can concentrate on specific form-motives and study their variations. Lastly, however, it is the experience of the oneness of genius one will gain from it. Of this the philosopher Konrad Fiedler, a contemporary of Cézanne, has written:

"It is the rare privilege of highly organized, sensitive persons that they can achieve immediate contact with nature. The relation to an object does not arise from single effects, on the contrary, they grasp its very existence, and they feel the object as a whole even before they break up this general feeling into many separate sensations. For such persons as these there is a pleasure and a delight in the vital experience of things far above such differences as the beautiful and the ugly." *On Judging Works of Visual Art*. Translated from the German by Henry Schaefer-Simmern and Fulmer Mood. Berkeley, University of California Press, 1949, p. 28.

CONTENTS

DRAWINGS

PAUL CEZANNE

WHEN PAUL CEZANNE ENTERED THE FIELD OF PAINT ing, he did not find a unified language of art as any young artist of previous centuries would have done, but a two-fold level of expression. On the one hand there was the officially recognized academic art, "the art of the schools," as the Impressionists disparagingly called it; on the other hand there was the art for the initiated, the connoisseurs, the advanced minds. In this typical nineteenth century situation, the young artist—in spite of and because of his conservative, small-town upbringing—immediately chose the advanced position. From Courbet, then in the last decade of his true productivity, he learned the power of plastic form, achieved by a modification of color, and color alone without the interference of line, the instrument of Ingres and the academic school. From Manet, making his first appearance with *The Breakfast in the Open* in 1863, he got "l'art pour l'art," an art with no other tendency but to cultivate its own means, and the broadest brushwork ever seen in French painting. But at the same time he absorbed with insatiable hunger the "old masters," primarily the great colorists Titian, Veronese, Tintoretto, Rubens, and their modern heir, Delacroix. In this interest he differed totally from the young naturalistic painters. In his youthful enthusiasm he wanted to emulate his great predecessors, but what he gained from this contact was a lasting insight into the significance of form. He discovered "nature rather late in life," and became in his own words: "an impressionistic painter." In the last part of his life, he succeeded in a synthesis of naturalism and pure form which seems like a crowning of the endeavors of painting in his century. This synthesis came as much from the spontaneous view under which life and nature appeared to him, as it derived from the tenacious and desperate struggle for "realization" of his sensory impressions. The spontaneous part of this creativity emerges from a person at once enthusiastic and timid, sensuous and ascetic, irritable and hardy, revolutionary and conservative. If one peruses his life story, one would hardly expect an oeuvre so consequent in its slow but steady growth, so keen and magnificent in its final accomplishments.

Yet beyond the eccentric personality of Cézanne, whose vexations compelled him to exclaim in desperation at the heights of his abilities "I am a man who does not exist," there worked this mysterious creative compulsion which seems to use a human being merely as an instrument for its fulfilment. In the religious language of his times Albrecht Duerer called this creative coercion "outpourings from above" (*oebere Eingiessungen*), while Cézanne, at the end of his life, wrote in a letter to Vollard: "Is art really a priesthood that demands the pure in heart

13

who must belong to it entirely"? What appeared to Duerer as an inspiration of Grace, was experienced by Cézanne as a monstrous but inevitable sacrifice of all that makes for happiness in life. In both instances the creative necessity operated beyond the biographical incidents. As an old man, however, it sometimes became clear to Cézanne toward what new horizons the creative force had directed him. He could say rightly to his young friend Gasquet "Perhaps I was born too early. I was more the painter of your generation than of mine."

Today one tends to emphasize the "abstract" factors so strongly evident in his later work, and one likes to quote from his letters to Bernard that one should "treat nature by the cylinder, the sphere, the cone"; however, one should not forget to add from the second part of his statement, "but nature for us men is more depth than surface." Corporeality and space appeared to Cézanne as the agents of cylinder, sphere, and cone, and with bewildering manifoldness the sensations of light enveloped the material structure of the world. The complexity of his vision, spread out between nature and abstraction, lends to each of his paintings the character of either a heroic struggle for harmonization or the serene and monumental finality of the accomplished image. Gauguin's flat surfaces as well as Van Gogh's ecstatic brushwork seemed to him fragmentary solutions on which "one should turn one's back," while Monet, representing the Impressionists, was "only an eye, but, good Lord, what an eye." Painting to him was neither the rendering of optical impressions "seen through a temperament" (Zola), nor the creation of a decorative symbolism (Gauguin), nor the deliverance of a passionate self (Van Gogh), but rather the gradual distillation of passions, optical sensations, physical shapes, and the organization of designs into images as much detached from the maker as from the motive in which they originated. They were, in his words, "constructions after nature, based on method, sensations, and developments suggested by the model." If "construction" and "method" were the terms hardly used in the vocabulary of the Impressionists, the object, nevertheless, remained the fountainhead of all his sensations and insights. To Cézanne, seeing was an act of discovery, which held the joy of revelation and the agony of denial. Nature revealed itself to him with such intensity that he could write, "The same subject seen from a different angle gives a subject for study of the highest interest and so varied, I think, I could be occupied for months without changing my place, simply bending a little to the right or the left." This preoccupation with seeing, permits us to define Cézanne's place in relationship to twentieth century art. The painter was admired by his naturalistic Impressionist friends such as Renoir, Pissarro, and Monet; he was venerated by the following generation of anti-naturalists and decorative symbolists such as Gauguin, Emile Bernard, and Maurice Denis and he was claimed as the father of cubism at the occasion of the Cézanne Memorial Exhibition in 1907. The final acclaim of the lonely master by three succeeding generations,

14

one representing the end stage in the evolution of naturalistic painting, the other transitional to abstract art, and the last completely novel and revolutionary, can only be explained by the comprehensiveness of Cézanne's style. It is based on a naturalistic view of the world; it is raised to the level of an art of order in space; and it points toward a victory of abstract form over its material sources. Cézanne never had in mind a renunciation of the visible world as the fountainhead of creation, and the paintings of Braque and Picasso would have been incomprehensible to him. Like the beam of a lighthouse, his art lit up the landscape of the future, but the source of such light remained confined by the sphere of his own time.

"Constructions after nature" were his aim, and his is undoubtedly the broadest artistic vision given to anybody in his century. What he could actually do, however, was confined by the limitations of his personality and of his age. Cézanne was not an especially skillful artist. He was not so able a draftsman as Degas. Nor for a long time could he translate his color sensations as freely and graciously onto the canvas as his Impressionist friends. He apparently was hampered also by seeing too much. Even in the last year of his life he wrote to his son, "I cannot attain the intensity that is unfolded before my senses. I have not the magnificent richness of colouring that animates nature." But on account of the breadth of his vision, and the experience of the slowness of its "realization," he distrusted mere skill and technique. "I believe in the logical development of everything I see and feel through the study of nature and turn my attention to technical questions later; for technical questions are for us only the means of making the public feel what we feel ourselves and making ourselves understood."

Thus, art was to him primarily the experience of creation, or as he called it "realization," and only secondarily communication. That this communicating power was in him less developed than the creative vision of nature, makes for one of the limiting features of his art. But it also makes his work so moving in its struggle for perfection.

One should expect the intrusion in his work of his own unbalanced, and in his later life, basically discontented personality. There is, however, nothing of that sort to be discovered. The obvious distortions in his art derive occasionally from awkwardness, more frequently from the nature of his aesthetic vision. Subjectivity is altogether absent. In the encounter with the visible world and in the act of expressing it, the painter Cézanne was able to absorb the man Cézanne, and put to service exclusively the constructive elements of his nature.

To some extent the realization of Cézanne's vision was, however, hampered by the period in which he lived. He was educated in the classical traditions of the Lycée, and it was from there that the literary and aesthetic inheritance of the past remained a living agent of his growth. The personal and novel way in which he saw the world, remained saturated with the patrimony of the European her-

15

itage. From this background stems his youthful endeavor to emulate his admired teachers, and from this derive the efforts of his old age "to do the old masters over again" in the large canvases of his *Bathers*. Cézanne felt that naturalistic painting was lacking to some extent in method and meaningfulness. To achieve these qualities, his own period offered him neither a living religion nor a living myth, neither an ideal concept of the human form nor an elegiac or pastoral image of nature. The imaginative and symbolic sources of art had run dry. This vacuum, not entirely filled by the freshness and precision of the naturalistic vision of his literary and painter friends, can also be felt in the portraits and in the "ideal scenes" of the master. The portraits are not animated by a social or humane concept as were those of the Renaissance, and his "classical" compositions suffer primarily from being born into an unmythical age. Some of his "bathers" therefore wear bathing trunks.

Cézanne's limitations do not diminish his stature. They only show him as a person born into time and place, stirred by their resistance to a heroic effort to realize an entirely original and complete vision of the world. This vision is spread out before us in more than a thousand paintings, watercolors, and drawings. In these works the broadest concept of the "language of forms" that the history of painting has known, is applied to and extracted from the visible. Cézanne has returned to us the material of the world as an organic universe. This world is silent, impenetrable, and luminous.

THE DRAWINGS AND WATERCOLORS

"Up to his last day he drew or painted for one hour, like a priest reading his breviary, *The Flayed Man* by Michelangelo from all its aspects. And I remember with what respect he evoked the image of Père Ingres, more than sixty years old, and walking daily under his umbrella, to the Louvre exclaiming: "I must learn how to draw." (Joachim Gasquet, Cézanne, Paris, new edition, 1926, p. 33) .

The work of Cézanne, the untiring draftsman, consists today of several hundred drawings never shown during his lifetime and infrequently displayed or published afterwards. Widely dispersed in the print rooms of museums and in private collections, they are not as much part of our awareness as the accomplished drawings of Ingres or Degas. There are also a number of sketch books (see bibliography) which permit an insight into the working process of the artist. Finally there are about four hundred watercolors, ranging from first denotations to finished pieces. They belong mostly to the epoch after 1890[1] when he preferred this technique to avoid carrying his painting equipment to the motive. A few years after his death, the first exhibition of his watercolors surprised the world with this unknown aspect of his oeuvre.[2]

Cézanne at various occasions, mostly in his letters, expressed his ideas about

16

drawing. They have been assembled by John Rewald in an article (*"Cézanne's Theories About Art," Art News,* November, 1948, p. 31, ff.) so that they need not be repeated. The artist was not a theoretician but he was capable of expressing more or less clearly what appeared to him important as a painter. It is understandable that the accent shifted according to the period and occasionally the mood, and it is therefore impossible to develop a unified system from his written and spoken remarks. Yet his statements are always so genuine that they cannot be discarded. In the field of drawing he tends to disparage the importance of line drawing. This is contradicted to some extent by his incessant use of linear denotation as a draftsman. The essential point is made in a letter to the young, inquisitive painter Emile Bernard: "Drawing and painting are not different things. To the degree that one paints, one draws. The more the color becomes harmonious, the more the line becomes precise" (Emile Bernard, *Souvenirs sur Paul Cézanne,* Paris, 1912. p. 35). This is entirely true for Cézanne because it marks the unique feature of his art: that he developed all means of expression simultaneously. The design emerged together with the color, and the color received its definition by linear demarcation. In tuning all forms of appearance: space and plane, light and color, color and line, to a common denominator, he could not, from his point of view, emphasize the part which drawing played in his work. While drawing to him was only a preparatory activity, for us it is an avenue of approach to his work. Beginning with the haphazard denotations on a sketch book page (Plate 14) or the scribblings on an old engraving (Plate 13), we can proceed to the visual explorations of his sketch books, until we arrive at compositional arrangements (Plates 11 and 20) which precede the execution in watercolor or oil. The sketch is rarely "sketchy." Even in his youthful, passionate jottings one perceives a relationship to a larger entity. In the later drawings the emphasis on the compositional context yields to an inherent adjustment to underlying form structures, such as the famous "cone, sphere, and cylinder," or to the directional orientation.

The watercolors are mostly large in size, sparing in medium, light in color. Their imitative function is reduced to a minimum, their suggestive power raised to a maximum. The composition differs by its organized balance from that of the Impressionists; their color, however, owes its range to their chromatic scale. Yet the color of Cézanne, derived from the sunlight palette, does not refer primarily to atmospheric values but to color intensities (th. i. local color modified by light) in relationship to their location on the picture plane and their recession in space. It is therefore of a much more abstract nature and establishes in cooperation with the white paper ground a reality free of its material weight. Within these watercolors there exists a wide range. Besides the drawings with only touches of color, there are the completely executed ones, in which the dried color is overlaid with new layers, thus creating a transparent and luminous surface in which the patches do not necessarily follow the demarcations of line. Although this is a rather slow procedure, the final result shows a lightness and ease which realizes the highest possibilities of this medium. The color is not attached to an object but rather hovers over the linear demarcations, so that it refers to a multiplicity of phenomena: it is color and light and local tone at once. Being unattached, it remains fluid and seems to float over the white ground of the paper like a cloud.

In both, drawing and watercolor, we notice the weakening of the dictates of physical nature and the gradual ascendancy of form-reality over nature-reality. Or in the words of Bernard: "His optics were more in his brain than in his eyes" (*op. cit.* p. 27).

THE NUDE

When young Paul Cézanne attended the Ecole des Beaux Arts in Aix between 1858 and 1861, his instructor, Joseph Gibert, may have quoted to him the saying of the God of all European art academies, Jean Dominique Ingres: "Even the smoke must be expressed by lines." What he meant by this, was that even the most vaporous phenomena should be raised to the dignity of definition by a linear circumscription. Such an approach was held to be "classical" and the academies considered themselves heirs to the great heritage of the Graeco-Roman spirit, revived by Raphael and the Carraccis. Cézanne's first drawings of nudes also reveal the cool discipline of the neo-classical training (Plate 1). Studies from life nudes guided the apprentice toward an understanding of static poses, while the copying of casts[3] impressed upon him the classical standards of "absolute" beauty. Cézanne, who had received a second prize in drawing at the Lycée in 1858, did as well as any reasonably talented and hard working art student. The few surviving examples show an appropriate use of line definition and light gradation achieved with lead or brush applied to a properly understood anatomy. The poses were well balanced and dignified and another artistic heir of Raphael could have been sent into the world to acquire prizes and public commissions. Does the second drawing of a nude (Plate 2), executed during the same period, indicate that, free from supervision, he was aiming at a direct expression in opposition to the style taught at the Academy, or is it simply a preparatory step before "the Line of Beauty" was laid over the first sketch, as we can observe it so frequently in the drawings of David? We do not know, but it is certain that the drawing—and there are others of the same type (V. 1164-1175, 1580, 1581)—shows a greater understanding of the muscular and bone structure of the human body than his later nudes. How much did he unlearn intentionally? How much did he, who rarely consulted the live model, forget?

18

How much did he sacrifice to the modifying forces of his "style"? These are puzzling questions which will constantly haunt the observer of Cézanne's drawings.

The virility of his line is further developed in his *Rowing Men* (Plate 3) which points toward the ideals of another Provençal draftsman, Daumier. The brisk denotation of the expressive rhythm of foreward leaning bodies turns away from the academic tradition of Raphael toward that of Michelangelo.[4] Now the human body is rather understood as the carrier of vital energies than as the most harmonious plant of creation. These energies are hardly retained in the bulging and flowing contour. Cézanne has already renounced defining his bodies by lines before they could define themselves by their own masses. This vigorous style is paralleled in his paintings of the same period by the use of the palette knife for the application of a heavy color paste, equalizing the experience of weighty matter with the use of materially substantial color. Drawing and painting both strive to escape an anemic concept of beauty and tend toward an aggressive truthfulness. This tendency stands behind the astounding drawings for *The Autopsy* (Plates 4 and 26). Like Caravaggio in the seventeenth century, Cézanne, further encouraged by the example of Courbet, challenges by his plastic materialism the representatives of an impotent idealism. At the same time this new directness is put into the service of excited visions: murder, rape, and temptation as subject matter seek for an adequate pictorial form. Cézanne finds it in Veronese, Tintoretto, Rubens, and Delacroix. The coloristic opulence of the Venetian art of the late Renaissance, the plastic energy of the Flemish, and the nostalgic afterglow of the Baroque in the French master excited Cézanne all his life. This Baroque tendency appears in his drawings in form of an undulating line which translates static forms into moving bodies. How much this style owes to his admired Delacroix may be seen by a comparison with an oil sketch of the older master executed for the *Study for the Apollo Ceiling of the Louvre* (Coll. Jaques Seligmann, New York) (Plate A). Cézanne actually made a copy of the river god prostrate to the left, but, more important, the entire vocabulary of forms of his nudes shows the absorption of Delacroix's concepts. This Baroque line remains a latent element in Cézanne's art to be evoked whenever the subject matter is related to "ideal" themes.

The foremost of these literary as well as traditional ideas is that of a configuration of bathing people such as Correggio and Domenichino had introduced for the glorification of an Arcadian marriage between man and nature. Ever since Manet had taken up this subject matter in 1863, Cézanne felt its challenge. In every decade of his life after 1870 he approached the theme again and the last photo of the painter shows him in front of a colossal canvas of the *Bathers*.[5] Like a recurring dream the happiness of youthful romping in the waters of the Arc river, as he illustrates it in a letter to Zola in 1859,[6] is to be awakened anew in the bather compositions. Here the unity between man and nature had to be regained as it existed in the full blooded creations of the past. And here the link was to be established between the contemporary analysis of nature and the classical tradition of the nude. "Poussin entirely redone upon nature," as the artist described it.[7] The selection of this book contains a number of such bather drawings, in which the poses of men and women are explored in view of their later incorporation into larger compositions (Plates 9, 15 and 16). Someone who knew only the artist's still lifes and later landscapes could hardly identify the author of these sketches. While aspiring to life likeness, the bodies nevertheless appear like memory images. In them the experience of reality seems fused with the after images of classical compositions. This recalls the situation of Delacroix and Daumier, in whom also the naturalistic material was instinctively adjusted to their stylistic formula. Nature provided the words, style cast them into sentences. This search for an organization of the sense-given data and their recreation into a classical idyl is paralleled in the same years by a great German, Hans von Marées.[8] His nudes, although based on a much greater knowledge of the human body, tend also toward a silhouette as the result of the inner physical energies moving centrifugally. A nude for his murals at the Aquarium in Naples from 1873, may serve for comparison (Plate B).

Besides the "adjusted" nature studies there exist a large number of free copies of individual figures from "classical" compositions as well as highly personal interpretations after paintings of the past. Cézanne liked to put on his walls reproductions of masterpieces. Plate 21 is done after a Signorelli drawing for the Orvieto murals. He is intrigued by Signorelli for the same reason for which he had turned to Michelangelo in Plate 15. The athletic prowess cast in a rhythmical order, the outward pressing masses defined by an expressive contour—this appeared to Cézanne's eye as a perfection which had to be regained from a completely fresh experience of nature. Compositional studies after Caravaggio (Plate 17), Rubens (Plate 10) and Delacroix (Plate 18) were all done from engravings or photographs, sharpening the artist's eyes for moving shapes in interaction. In a later period of his life incessant drawing from sculpture permitted him to experience an already pre-styled reality such as a live model would never yield. Cézanne thoroughly worked his way through the collection of casts in the Louvre (today in the Trocadéro), with no observable stylistic predilections. Sculptures from antiquity, the Renaissance, the Baroque, and the nineteenth century were chosen for adoption into his pictorial memory. Plate 22 represents such a study after Donatello's St. George in Or' San Michele. Yet now at the height of his ability, the model is expressed entirely in terms of Cézanne's own style. With a Greco-like elongation the stolid forms of the Renaissance hero are turned into new and expressive shapes. The angle is chosen in such a way that the left arm appears as the continuation of the

20

ascending forms of the shield, with the result that the entire figure seems to repeat the lozenge design. Parallel lines behind the figure invigorate the axial directions. In this drawing we witness for the first time the most typical occurrence in the mature work of the artist—the interaction between nature image and geometry, between sensory experience and formal organization. In spite of its distortions Cézanne has come closer to the essence of Donatello's statuesque art than any precise copy. The painter owned himself two casts, one after Puget's *Amor,* the other after Houdon's *Flayed Man (L'Ecorché).* He never tired of studying them and incorporated them into several of his paintings. The compulsion to draw in order to make the object a part of himself was heightened here by an innate sympathy with the Provençal Baroque of Puget that had been with him since childhood. Certainly Cézanne has overcome the dead surface of the cast and given us the sculptural quality of the original by his rippling and rising silhouette (Plate 19). The *Study After Houdon's Ecorché* (Plate 25) is stylistically related to the study after Donatello. It presents the same extreme elongation and small head, held together by a silhouette echoing the tension of the statue. The central importance of this model has been pointed out in the catalogue section.

Thus fortified with countless studies after engravings, photos, paintings and sculptures, yet always avoiding the live model as much as possible, Cézanne could approach configurations of several figures. The earliest example is from the same period in which the artist painted his most naturalistic landscapes (Plate 11). While the distribution of the masses of light and dark, the spacing of the figures and the consonance of human forms and nature forms indicate the maturity of Cézanne's sense of form, the nudes are rendered with a strange vagueness of action as if the artist could not decide what pose to give them. In the Renaissance the composition emerges from the active and passive poses of the individual participants in their mutual relationship; here the idea of the whole seems to be preordained in the mind and must now be realized by invented figures. The result remains tentative but tense with the promises of an unobtainable fulfilment. Related to this drawing is the watercolor of *Bathers* (Plate 20) in which the lightness of the color scheme seems to free the motive from its origin in obsessive phantasmagorias and to transfer it to an impersonal serenity. The contact with his earlier style is still discernible in the squat proportions and curved lines. In the choice of this subject matter the artist pursues a nostalgic dream—the classical idyl—that he shares with a few of his contemporaries. Renoir during the same period painted this motive several times and Fantin Latour, a dreamer of beauty in conventional forms, has left us a comparable drawing (Museum Lille, repr. in René Huyghe, *French Drawings of the 19th Century,* London, 1956, No. 97). Yet closest in spirit to Cézanne comes again Hans von Marées *Hesperides* (Staatsgalerie, Munich), in which we find a similarly majestic but also fragmentary creation. These nudes give expression to the longing of the nineteenth-century artist to recapture a synthesis between man and the earth such as Giorgione had first celebrated. It shows Cézanne too in search of "the long and perfect interaction between the ideal form remembered and natural appearances observed, which is the foundation of all great drawings from Michelangelo to Degas" (Kenneth Clark, *The Nude*, New York, 1956, p. 218).

Manet's *Breakfast in the Open* had helped Cézanne to gain access to the fundamental idyl of the *Bathers*. Manet's *Olympia* stirred the artist to find form for his passionate erotic images. It might surprise one to discern in the work of the most objective master of the last century, Cézanne, a shadow world of sexual demons. It is because of his passionate character that the artist distrusted the world and himself and turned to things that could not—as he used to say—"put a hook" on him. Among the most unbridled compositions is that of the so called *Afternoon at Naples* (V. 223, 224, 822), showing a nude couple served by a Negro servant. Plate 5 is a preparatory sketch for it. The hurrying lines are entirely born from a visionary condition which has taken shape under the spell of Delacroix's *Death of Sardanapal*. The thrusting diagonal forms of his Baroque compositions are condensed into two bodies, disquieting in their deformation. Rushing lines float over the paper echoing the main forms. Cézanne, in his mid-twenties, appears closer to El Greco and Kokoschka than to his own later work. Plate 8 is one of several watercolors in which a direct, although probably ironical, tribute is paid to Manet's *Olympia*. That Cézanne must have seen in this composition a challenge to the world—and probably to himself—can be concluded from the fact that he exhibited an even more hectic version of the subject (V. 225), with his own portrait as Olympia's admirer included, at the first Impressionist exhibition. The watercolor is more tranquil, and obviously in search of the modern, erotic idyl. The feminine rounded forms suggest the curvilinear rhythm which dominates the design. Eyeless and faceless as nearly all figures of his erotic compositions, the inward-born idea without the nourishment of things actually seen and experienced, dictate the presentation. Cézanne at this time was not yet decided to become a painter of the real world. Often he must have felt himself closer to Delacroix and Daumier than to Manet and Pissarro. What unrecorded struggle lies behind his renunciation of the *Modern Olympia* in favor of the still lifes and landscapes! It is primarily as their interpreter that he has entered the memory of mankind.

PORTRAITS

In his portraits Cézanne moves in an intermediary zone between literary subject matter and the objective data of still lifes and landscapes. The very fact that Cézanne did portraits throughout his life suggests that he saw in his sitters more than "nature morte" as some writers have inferred. It is rather that during the process of painting, the artist became so absorbed in the formal aspects of his picture that the human element receded. Besides his innate difficulty in associating with his fellow-beings—the earmark of many great creators—established a distance between himself and the sitter. Yet who can judge how much this distance was necessary to achieve his aims? The neutral poses and the faces "beyond good and evil"—"cardplayers" without the spirit of play, "Harlequins" without laughter—present, in fact, a new image of man. In the words of Martin Buber: "The creative imagination is according to its innermost nature discovery through image making" ("Der Mensch und sein Gebilde" *Neue Rundschau*, 1955, I, 12). While his portraits are not exploratory of human emotions as in Delacroix, nor of the plastic sensations of never before observed movements, as in Degas, nor expressions of sensual sympathy, as in Renoir, they create human creatures as selfcontained entities in the visible universe. Their immobility is that of a concentrated presence.

Cézanne's sketch books are filled with likenesses of his wife, his son, his parents, his sister, and of himself. In addition, we have the drawings of his friend Pissarro (Plates 28, 29, and 30), of his dealer Vollard (Plate 46), of the peasants who modelled for *The Cardplayers* (Plates 42 and 43), of the youthful model for the *Boy with the Red Vest* (Plate 45), and of his gardener Vallier (Plate 48). These sketchbook drawings are often mere denotations without reference to any intended composition. They are, therefore, mostly concentrated head-studies, with an occasional glimpse of the figure of the model taken unaware. The earliest in this group is the sketch *Cézanne's Father Reading a Newspaper* (Plate 27) related to the painting of the same subject matter (V. 91) of the period 1868-70. The zestful line recalls Daumier, Gavarni, and other draftsmen of the 1850's. In comparison the few lines and parallel shadow strokes in the drawing of *The Father of the Artist* (Plate 40) executed in the 1880's seem so organized. Innumerable times he captured the likeness of his beloved son Paul who throughout his life was to be his closest friend, adviser, and agent. With a few lines he denotes the rounded, eager face (Plates 38 and 39), and the very fact that we can apply to it a description of mood, indicates a personal participation by the artist. There are several drawings of Cézanne's wife, his .most patient model, in our selection. Plate 35 is exceptional because of the soft, luminous treatment of the surface, which lends the unusual element of mood. The drawing shows the same diagonal slant which we observe in the more developed pieces (Plates 36 and 37). Where little Paul's head presents the roundness of a billiard ball, Mme. Cézanne's features are given in a pure oval. This organizing presence of an axial direction and of basic geometrical shapes points out that even in the intimate and personal sketch the familiarity with the sitter cannot distract from his fundamental issue—the creation of an ordered pictorial universe derived from nature. Therefore the evolution from an accidental sketch (Plate 36) to the great portrait of *Mme. Cézanne in the Conservatory* (V. 569) is a completely logical one. Organization exists from the initial drawing as a condition of the aesthetic reality of the image.

The sequence of self portraits in this volume (Plates 31, 32, 33, and 34) is in itself a story of human fascination upon which we have commented in our catalogue section. Like Duerer and Rembrandt, Cézanne paid unceasing attention to his own features. Not only was he his own indefatigable model, but we are inclined to believe that he felt as intrigued as his great predecessors by the "self," the mysterious fountainhead of the creative impetus operating through him.

The elimination of action remains the earmark of all of his portraits to the very end. And yet some of the late portraits show the same intensification which we shall observe in his still lifes and landscapes. *Boy with the Red Vest* (Plate 45) is a preparatory sketch for four of the greatest of his portraits, all of them done between 1890 and 1895. In general, youthful models are absent in the painter's work. The more surprising therefore to find in this drawing such heightened vitality, expressed by agitated brush lines and loose patches of color. In fluid motion the forms of the long hair glide down into the red vest—the evocative coloristic center—and reassemble in the area of the hands. Since the immobile head is half effaced by patches of greenish color, the physiognomical expressiveness derives entirely from the nearly furious execution. This contrast between a hieratic motionless frontality and the sweeping rush of lines gives this portrait its haunting depth. *The Gardener Vallier* (Plate 48), one of the old men whom Cézanne painted in coeval sympathy, presents the very opposite characteristics. The pencil lines touch only lightly the paper, the color patches, rendering the greenness of a gardener's world, are transparent. Like a halo converging at his straw hat trees enclose the model. And again, in spite of its neutral pose, a contemplative and serene mood is evoked, making the gardener one of "the Confraternity of the Wooden Shoes of God" (Balzac, *Père Goriot*). It is as if Cézanne were gazing through the crystalline order of his world and seeing it become transparent and dissolve again in the great, unending stream of all life. A touch of the immaterial, a feeling of abandon has moved the old painter.

STILL LIFES

The still life is in some ways the most adequate theme for Cézanne's art. It permits the painter to compose forms and space and color relations with objects

24

which are already endowed with shapes. His objects are indeed "nature morte" and cannot irritate an artist in search of the unchangeable. What they lack in the animation of a human model, they yield in the concentrated display of pure form. That Cézanne was not interested in the perfume of flowers, in the lusciousness of his fruits, or in the texture of his jars, is evident. This is surprising for one living so intimately with vegetative nature. On the other hand, Cézanne displayed the keenest ingenuity in the arrangement of these still lifes.[9] The selection of objects, the juxtaposition of occasionally the most incongruous things, is exclusively guided by considerations of form. Already in his earliest still lifes, such as the *Black Clock* (V. 69), the objects take on an austere intensity which cannot be explained by their formal values alone. The world of things loses its man-serving connotations and the objects are returned to us as if we had never seen them before. With indescribable intensity "the Thing" insists on being. Yet its existence is not that of its subservient function in life but its roundness, its hardness, its exposure to light, its relation to other objects, its direction in the angle of presentation. Just because it is all form, it seems to reveal new experiences of reality. As in the fugues of Bach, where the organization of sounds is underlaid by emotion "a priori" (emotion as such), here emotion underlies the organization of forms.

Before we enter into a discussion of the drawings and watercolors of still lifes, i.e. of configurations of objects, we select a few drawings of isolated objects. The study of such objects was as much due to his fascination with them as by his desire to bring about a form-image that paralleled the object in its essential features. In this sense the drawings after Baroque and Rococo ornaments are especially fascinating. The *Ornament in the Style of Louis XIV* (Plate 53) and the *Rococo Clock* (Plate 52) show that Cézanne's adolescent love for the Baroque remained with him as a conservative-Aix-tradition to his late years. The drawings recreate the rhythmical flow of the Baroque line in a bilateral controlled motion of the hand around a middle axis. And yet Cézanne's imprint is as well defined as El Greco's. The circular forms stretch and tend toward the oval. An expressive elongation, partially in response to the oblong shape of the sketch book, transforms them in character.

Although Cézanne subordinated line to color in his paintings, here we can observe the artist in his training for the primary definition of objects. *Six Apples* (Plate 59) may be compared to the short chromatic exercises of Bach. The number of apples varies in the numerous renditions of the subject. Each time a new organism—a oneness of changing parts—emerges. The circular motion of the hand brings about the final form, essence of an apple, a spherical shape. Its core is inert, its circumference active. Where two spheres meet, the motion is taken up and carried further. A stellar constellation of orbs appears. In *Three Pears* (Plate 54), a completely finished watercolor, the rhomboid shapes are conceived in consonance with the shape of the platter, the Baroque curve of the table's edge, and the sprays of wall paper. Still life as a plastic ornament! In the *Hortensias* (Plate 62) the landscape of a potted flower and a curtain rises as a pyramidal structure, while in the *Oranges on a Platter* (Plate 61) the rhythmical consonance of spherical forms in motion is set against the rigid and static immobility of straight, vertical lines. In reality, how could a single fruit, set apart from the platter, acquire such an intensity? Since aesthetic formulation can stir the entirety of our experiences and responses, distance, apartness can take on emotional quality. The *Still life with Bottles, Pots, and Alcohol Stove* (Plate 60) represents Cézanne's discovery of form configurations on its most complex level. While the previous examples were all laid out on a horizontal and developed on the lower third of the paper, here the entire picture surface is rhythmically, plastically, and spatially organized. The cone, the sphere, and the cylinder, quoted by the artist as the underlying structure of nature, are discovered in bottles and jars, and juxtaposed in the same manner in which related sounds are grouped for the emergence of a new entity—the melody. In this instance Cézanne's melody is austere, clipped, on the borderline between harmony and dissonance. It is this peculiarly modern syncopation which made Braque and Picasso paint their early cubistic arrangements in the spirit of this still life.

Yet as in the case of the late, passionate landscapes there exist besides the "classical" still lifes a number of "Baroque" ones (and the reader is at liberty to call them "romantic" or "expressionistic"). Their character rests on the prevalence of flowing, rounded, and dynamic forms, expressive of a subjective and passionate spirit. Sometimes the instigation must have been merely formal, an exploration of spherical shapes. In the *Still Life with Eggplant, Pomegranates, a Sugar Bowl, and a Carafe on a Table* (Plate 55), the artist has selected a number of objects of bulbous shape and has placed them without interval on a diagonally receding plane. In the hands of a lesser master this would have resulted in an ugly and inert composition. With Cézanne it is music in a new key, unknown, intriguing, exploratory. This is also true for the watercolor *Still life with Soup Bowl and Bronze Goblet* (Plate 56). In the catalogue we have discussed the strange associations related with this late work. Does it not connect in form and spirit with the passionate effusions of his early years; instead of order and clarity, the transformation of the visible world into a vision aflame? Not Braque and Picasso, but Soutine and Kokoschka seem anticipated in this watercolor. The past has remained with Cézanne and from time to time in old age the experiences of youth return to him. They speak of the fact that Cézanne's "classical" art is the fruit of a long and arduous process. This is probably what Cézanne meant in pointing out the central importance of the artist's temperament for his creation.[10]

The very subject of still lifes and landscapes permits an artist to forget himself or, at least, to objectify his personal experiences in the mute readiness of an already existent world. Nature presents itself in plastic forms, in colors, in atmospheric modification, and in spatial relationships. Its precreated configuration of shapes and colors can guide him toward an aesthetic order without personal involvement. It is, in fact, Cézanne who has helped us through his all-embracing approach to realize the totality of these factors. In Courbet the plastic forms had emerged from their coloristic definition, and in Impressionism from their atmospheric modification; in Cézanne a highly organized visible world came into being by a synthesis of all factors. Unsupported by any facility for execution, he held in readiness a unique sensibility, the application of which was guided by an infinitely complex and subtle aesthetic intelligence. Day by day this sensibility struggled with the organizing intelligence; he would not permit himself to put down a stroke without knowing its function within the general context. Vollard has told us of the excruciating portrait sessions in which he had to experience Cézanne's working procedures. It is this forcing together of the sensibility which registers the variety and subtlety of the outer world and the inner organizing intelligence which the artist described as "realization." In his Impressionist days, during the study with Pissarro in Pontoise identical motives executed by the friends show on the part of Cézanne a much greater determination to clarify his optical impressions by balancing mass and space, foreground and recession.

From this period date our first landscape drawings and watercolors. Their appearance is indicative of the trend away from the literary and imaginary toward the visible world as a subject matter. A certain predilection for architectural forms as buttresses for the composition is apparent. In this he differs from the Impressionists who shy away from any design that could emphasize geometrical patterns and thus break the vegetative-atmospheric ensemble. *Entrance Into a Garden* (Plate 65) with its idyllic mood, so unusual with the artist, anticipates the one executed probably a few years later (Plate 67). How strongly the latter establishes a uniform rhythm in which the eye cannot longer pick out individual forms. From enumeration to the total statement! Yet the total statement at this time is still made in terms of an atmospheric unification, such as in the surprising *Landscape near Mélun* (Plate 66), where the artist spent some time in 1877 and 1878. It is nearly with a feeling of shock that one accepts this rather brilliant Impressionist study as a work of Cézanne. Its summer richness of color, its happiness of deep space, cannot compensate for the relative absence of organization which seems to us an indispensable part of Cézanne's artistic language. More than that, suddenly we begin to understand that every later work of Cé-

27

zanne is developed from the smallest units toward the final result in one homo-genous process. Here the patches of color are descriptive of the objects in na-ture, but not constructive for the architecture of the total image. Even in the black and white reproduction the houses isolate themselves from the patch work of saturated colors in the foliage. They are stated as houses but not as forms. Compare with this the *House in Provence* (Plate 82), executed about fifteen years later. Without the technical brilliance of the previous watercolor, it gives us at one glance the togetherness of house and trees in their silent yet insistent existence. Instead of covering the entire paper with color and thus creating the Impressionist, vegetative-atmospheric web, the brush proceeds within a given key and indicates the intensity of local color modified by light rather than a description of the colored area in the object. This intensity is related to all the other intensities of color, which in themselves are determined by their position in the picture space. These colors range between a key color of blue and the whiteness of the paper in a chromatic rise from dark to light. On the opposite of the scale is ochre brown and between these three general levels the blue, the ochre, and the white, the local colors are set as in a scaffolding. Finally, the color patches are related to the basic whiteness of the paper, which stands for lum-inosity, for space, and for a binding atmospheric tone such as the blue color in his paintings. The white paper in all of his later watercolors appears as the ground of existence which holds all phenomena of nature together and lends them a density of reality which no naturalistic likeness can ever achieve. The Impressionists rendered the image of nature, Cézanne developed it from the germ to the final organism. Often in his later years the water color procedure with its fluid and suggestive manner influenced the execution of his oils. Or should we not better say that in both of them the same degree of concentration had been reached? It may also be noticed that the patches of color conform more to the plane of the paper than to the roundness or plasticity of the ob-jects. The spatial effect of color is nearly reduced to the forward or backward moving action of warm and cool tones, while the spatial description is given by the linear skeleton. The direction of the brush work sometimes follows this linear net, sometimes overlayes it. Lines are not drawn continuously and therefore are neither ornamental nor isolating. They appear like the borders of a river, but they do not stop the flow of the stream.

In observing the character of line in Cézanne's watercolors, we may ask for the general meaning of line drawing in his work.[11] He has repeatedly expressed his negative attitude toward line as an aesthetic value; he does not want to recog-nize it as existent in nature, nor as valid apart from color. This theoretical nega-tion is probably to be explained by his opposition to the linear art of the Acade-mies based on the traditions of Flaxman and Ingres, but it also conforms to the emphasis which the Impressionists put on the diffuseness of light and the

28

sketchiness of line. While Cézanne did not avail himself of the Impressionist means, his thinking was influenced by their point of view.

If we choose as an example of his mature style *The Village of L'Estaque* (Plate 71), we can clearly discern the function of drawing in his work. He nearly always uses pencil, rarely charcoal. This medium permits him to obtain a clear and sharp line rather than the intermittent residue of small particles of coal broken by the surface of the paper. While the latter lends itself to a soft mood (Millet, early van Gogh), to a characterization of textures (Watteau, Degas) or to the rendition of the play of light on solid form (Seurat), Cézanne is impervious to such possibilities. Line for him is first of all the denotation of a form in space. With a minimum of anticipation of those elements which will be entrusted to color, he designs a skeleton for future composition. Yet the accidental and the momentary, so stirring to Degas, are entirely absent. *L'Estaque* is not a nature sketch (one compares it with the earlier Plate 64 of the same subject), but from the very beginning a compositional sketch. The idea of order —the unchanging structure—is immediately extracted from nature. Therefore the inclination for cubic forms which organize the crystalline world of his images. Straight lines have replaced the wavy "Baroque" lines of his early period. They are not any longer the handwriting of emotions but rather the seismographic reactions of the descriptive hand. Without subjective emotion, the seemingly detached statement registers nevertheless his personality, brought by the act of creation into balance and harmony. What strikes us foremost in this drawing is the art of omission. These omissions not only leave out the accidental, but they prevent the isolation of objects from each other. In one continuous movement the eye of the observer proceeds over the entire surface. No direction is stressed, no effect is emphasized. The objects of nature are suspended in an equilibrium that reality itself can never offer to the eye.

This organizing intelligence is not only put in motion by the motive observed but also by the shape and the color of the painting ground—in this instance the white paper. One can study this especially well in his rendering of trees. The size of the trunks, the direction of the branches, is immediately modified by the format of the paper. In the *Landscape with Bare Trees* (Plate 72) the horizontal shape of the paper has brought about an emphasis on a horizontal sequence of lines opposed by the vertical of the tree trunks. In the sketch of a *Tree* (Plate 81) the trunk parallels the edge of the paper, and the longest branch is identical with the long horizontal of the paper. In *Trees and Houses* (Plate 75), the length of the trees is exaggerated because the form of the objects is adjusted to the dominant of the aesthetic reality—the painting ground. Never before Cézanne, and not after him, has there been such an interpenetration of the motive as a reality and the media of expression as the condition of its existence.

29

In the last phase of his work after 1890, a new type of landscape water-colors appears. Not only do preparatory studies in pencil become exceedingly rare, but the solidifying straight line disappears as a skeleton for the composition. In *The Turn of the Path* (Plate 89) the form is entirely given with the brush, avoiding any delimiting of silhouettes; the individual object is subordinate to a total vision of color. Slanting layers of changing density establish a coloristic vibration which, together with the curving path, create the image of an abandoned unity with nature. As in the work of old Titian and Rembrandt, the color sensations dissolve and at the same time unify the material world. Therefore the basic differentiations of a nature-related art, such as matter and space, foreground and background, become literally immaterial. In this sense the late paintings and water colors of Cézanne are his most personal, although not his most subjective works. In the same category belong *Pistachio Tree at Chateau Noir* (Plate 84), with its dramatic rhythm of curved shapes against the coercing power of crystalline forms and *Trees at the Water* (Plate 91), with its rhythmically modulated air- and waterspace in slanting vertical patches, echoing the diagonal and vertical shapes of trees. *Wall with Trees* (Plate 90) presents the highest possibility of a motive which we first observed in Plates 65 and 67. The reality of the scene is greater than in the earlier more descriptive statements. It confronts us with essences. Horizontals, diagonals, rhythmically spaced intervals, extract a basic experience of equilibrium in space. We partake in a harmony which speaks of finalities of our existence: space, light, growth, order.

Yet old Cézanne does not live in a universe of preordained harmony, and it would be a very wrong idea to imagine him as a serene Platonic thinker. Gasquet's descriptions of an infinitely gentle sage are moving documents of a youthful admiration, but the reality is much more complex. In the paintings and watercolors of the last decade a wild and feverish exaltation occasionally breaks through. He abandons the cultivated landscape of the Impressionists and turns to the wild pine forest, to lonely quarries (Plates 86 and 87), to the isolated and haunted scenery of *Chateau Noir* (Plate 88). This predilection for wild growth and lonely places is paralleled by the replacement of axial order and cubic form through long and sweeping curves which are carriers of the passionate involvement of the painter. Throughout his mature life Cézanne had painted and drawn over and over again the crowning mountain above the valley of the Arc River, Mont-Sainte-Victoire. Usually it is rendered from a distance, and the vast vista includes land, sea, and sky, held together by the polyphonous unity of his color. A few years before his death the painter approached this symbol of his Provencal existence from close by (Plate 92). The happiness of space disappears, the accidental shrinks to nothingness. With a few long drawn curves the barren grandeur of the mountain sweeps into existence—this barren grandeur which gives a suggestion of the lonely old man scaling the world down to its essentials.

The same predilection for lines in motion, taking the eye upward and down again, may be discovered in *The Balcony* (Plate 85). Who would have expected such a strongly linear drawing in so dedicated a colorist? Yet the line not only bespeaks his fascination with the design of the railing interpreted as curves in motion, it also sets the loose color patches in fluctuation. Close and nearly threatening, the objects in these last two watercolors express an ardent lyricism which made his later works as much a signal to twentieth century expressionism as it did to twentieth century cubism (see plates C and D).

Step by step, with anguish and anxiety, he had moved toward the realization of a new vision of the world. Now the language of forms employed with such indestructible density, has loosened and yields to the intangible. Art-form and nature-form have grown together. Violently, then tenderly, the earth surged up toward the painter. To hold what in itself was not any longer fixed and static, became the last of the never ending struggle. Of this he spoke to his young friend Gasquet: " 'I cannot tear my eyes away (from the object),' he told me one day. 'They are so totally glewed to the point which I view that they seem to bleed' " (Joachim Gasquet, Cézanne, p. 101). Through agony and abandon, the sap rises in these late watercolors to the crown. To know the completeness, the consoling grandeur of his vision was left to those who came after him.

NOTES

1) However, in 1867, Cézanne's friend Marion wrote to their companion, the musician Morstatt, from Aix: "His watercolors are particularly remarkable, their coloration amazing, and they produce a strange effect of which I did not think watercolors were capable. "John Rewald. *Paul Cézanne*, New York, 1948, p. 68. Venturi dates the earliest watercolors (V. 806-809) between 1865 and 1870. The earliest mention is in a letter to Emile Zola from June 30, 1866, in which he writes that he wants to buy a box of watercolors in order to work in this medium while he is not doing oil painting. (Paul Cézanne, *Correspondance*, Ed. John Rewald, Paris 1937, p. 96.)

2) At Bernheim-Jeune in Paris 1910.

3) Probably the earliest drawing by the artist is from the cast of a Hellenistic female torso. Repr. John Rewald, *op. cit*, fig. 12. It is done in the same manner as this nude.

4) This resentment against Raphael can still be felt in a letter of the old master. "Michel-Ange est un constructeur, et Raphael un artiste qui, si grand q'uil soit, est toujours bridé par le modèle" (*Correspondance*, p. 268).

5) Repr. John Rewald, *op. cit*. fig. 110.

6) Repr. *ibid.* p. 7. See also the reminiscence of Zola *ibid.* p. 5.

7) *Cézanne par ses lettres et ses témoins*, Ed. Bernard Dorival. Paris 1948, p. 192 (to Gasquet).

8) See the author: Hans von Marées and the classical doctrine in the nineteenth century (*Art Bulletin*, vol. XX, 1938, p. 291 ff).

9) See the description of Louis Le Bail in a letter (John Rewald, *op. cit*, p. 200–201).

10) *Correspondance*, letter to Bernard, July 25, 1904, p. 265.

11) See Fritz Novotny, "Cézanne als Zeichner," *Wiener Jahrbuch für Kunstgeschichte*, 1950, p. 225 ff.

SELECTED BIBLIOGRAPHY

General

JOHN REWALD (ed.), *Correspondance de Paul Cézanne*, Paris, 1937 (English translation by John Rewald, London, 1941).

BERNARD DORIVAL (ed.), *Cézanne par Ses Lettres et Ses Témoins*, Paris, 1948.

RAINER MARIA RILKE, *Briefe über Cézanne* (1907), Wiesbaden, 1952.

EMILE BERNARD, *Souvenirs sur Paul Cézanne*, Paris, 1912.

AMBROISE VOLLARD, *Cézanne*, Paris, 1914 (English translation by Harold van Doren, New York, 1937).

JOACHIM GASQUET, *Cézanne*, Paris, 1921 (new edition, 1926).

ROGER FRY, *Cézanne: A Study of His Development*, New York, 1927.

GERSTLE MACK, *Paul Cézanne*, New York, 1935.

LIONELLO VENTURI, *Cézanne: Son Art— Son Oeuvre*, Paris, 1936 (two volumes).

FRITZ NOVOTNY, *Cézanne*, London, 1937.

FRITZ NOVOTNY, *Cézanne und das Ende der Wissenschaftlichen Perspektive*, Vienna, 1938.

JOHN REWALD, *Cézanne: Sa Vie, Son Oeuvre, Son Amitié pour Zola*, Paris, 1939.

ERLE LORAN, *Cézanne's Composition*, Los Angeles, 1943.

JOHN REWALD, *Paul Cézanne: A Biography*, New York, 1948.

JOHN REWALD, "Cézanne's Theories About Art," *Art News*, November, 1948.

BERNARD DORIVAL, *Cézanne*, Paris, 1948.

MEYER SCHAPIRO, *Cézanne*, New York, 1952.

CURT BADT, *Die Kunst Cézannes*, Munich, 1956.

Drawings and Watercolors

JULIUS MEIER-GRAEFE, *Cézannes Aquarelle*, Munich, 1921.

MAURICE DENIS, "Le Dessin de Paul Cézanne," *L'Amour de l'Art*, February, 1924.

EMILE BERNARD, "Les Aquarelles de Paul Cézanne," *L'Amour de l'Art*, February, 1924.

LEON WERTH, "Dessins, Aquarelles de Cézanne," *L'Art Vivant*, May, 1924.

GEORGE WALDEMAR, *Cézanne: Aquarelles*, Paris, 1926.

A. SALMON, "Dessins Inedits de Cézanne," *Cahiers d'Art*, 1926.

ADRIEN CHAPPUIS, *Les Dessins de Paul Cézanne*, Paris, 1938.

CURT BADT, "Cézanne's Watercolor Technique," *Burlington Magazine*, October, 1943.

LIONELLO VENTURI, *Paul Cézanne Watercolours*, London, 1943.

GEORG SCHMIDT, *Watercolors by Paul Cézanne*, New York and Basle, n.d. (English translation by Glynn Hughes).

FRITZ NOVOTNY, "Cézanne als Zeichner," *Wiener Jahrbuch für Kunstgeschichte*, XIV, 1950.

JOHN REWALD (ed.). *Paul Cézanne Carnet de Dessins*, Paris, 1951 (two volumes).

CARL O. SCHNIEWIND (ed.), *Paul Cézanne Sketch Book* (owned by the Art Institute of Chicago), New York, 1951 (two volumes).

ADRIEN CHAPPUIS, *Dessins de Cézanne*, Lausanne, 1957.

CATALOGUE

NUDES

1 MALE NUDE, 1862

Pencil and wash. 610 x 470. Signed and dated on the back: Paul Cézanne 1862. Venturi 1162. Musée Granet, Aix-en-Provence. (Photo Henry Ely, Aix.)
From the same group as V. 1584 and V. 1627. Five more studies exist in the Ecole des Beaux Arts in Aix, where they were executed by the artist. It might be surprising to find so academic and so exacting a drawing in the work of Cézanne. However, it merely indicates that he underwent the same training as other young artists about 1860, and that his skill did not lag behind theirs. The quiet pose, the symmetrical silhouette, and the careful shading with a sharpened pencil point to the influence of the Ingres tradition. We remember that, during the same period, Cézanne did the panels of the *Four Seasons* for his parents' house and signed them in mocking envy, "Ingres."

2 NUDE MALE FIGURE SEEN FROM THE BACK, 1859-62

Pencil. 230 x 170. Venturi 1163. John N. Streep, New York. (Photo John D. Schiff, New York.)
Ctlg. *Paul Cézanne*, Den Haag, 1956, No. 92; Ctlg. *Paul Cézanne*, Munich, 1956, No. 111; Ctlg. *Paul Cézanne*, Kunsthaus Zurich, 1956, No. 145.
It is noteworthy that Cézanne in his early years drew the human body more correctly than in his later years. He still had access to the nude model, which he shunned later, and the question of "style" had not yet entered his mind. The result is a bold treatment of the human figure with the interest focused on a fluent contour and on muscular energy. The line—in opposition to his academic instruction—is intentionally unbeautiful, seeking for a virile expression. The next step is represented by *Rowing Men* (Plate 3).

3 ROWING MEN, 1865-70

Pencil. 227 x 229. Venturi 1175. Museum Boymans, Rotterdam.
Ctlg. *Paul Cézanne*, Den Haag, 1956, No. 93 (repr.); Ctlg. *Paul Cézanne*, Munich, 1956, No. 112 (repr.); Ctlg. *Paul Cézanne*, Kunsthaus, Zurich, 1956, No. 146, Fig. 66.
The drawing, with its robust and quick line and its effort to present the human body in motion, is related to the drawings *The Divers* (Plate 12) and *The Autopsy* (Plates 4 and 26). Already the the artist had left behind him the timid academic manner in the tradition of Ingres and released his curves which distantly recall the style of Daumier.

Three times Cézanne has caught the forward inclination of the rowers and translated it into a rhythmical design.

4 STUDY FOR "THE AUTOPSY," 1865-67

Charcoal on buff paper. 310 x 475. Not in Venturi. Mrs. Benny Goodman. Art Institute of Chicago.

John Rewald, *Paul Cézanne*, New York, 1948, Fig. 13; Ctlg. *Paul Cézanne,* Art Institute of Chicago, Metropolitan Museum of Art, New York, 1952, No. 8 repr.). Adrien Chappuis, *Dessins de Cézanne,* Lausanne, 1951, No. 3 (1867-69).

Study for the painting *The Autopsy* (V. 105). (See also Plate 26). Inscription by the artist with names and address in the right upper corner. The forms of the outstretched legs are repeated above the actual drawing. The lines are heavy and undifferentiated; the shadows follow the contour and block it in. The brutal ugliness of the arrangement of the corpse and the strong handling of the material show the artist flaunting the complacency of an already accepted academic style. In the final composition of the painting, a certain grotesque grandeur emerges which may have been stimulated by the study of Caravaggio-like Baroque compositions representing the *Deposition of Christ.*

5 STUDY FOR "L'APRES-MIDI A NAPLES," 1872-73

Black chalk. 140 x 290. Venturi 1176 (only the left upper section). Kupferstichkabinett der Offentlichen Kunstsammlung, Basle (inv. 1934. 212).

Ctlg. *Paul Cézanne,* Den Haag, 1956, No. 97 (repr.); Ctlg. *Paul Cézanne,*

Kunsthaus, Zurich, 1956, No. 151, Fig. 67.

The sketches V. 1176-1183 all relate to the paintings V. 223 and V. 224, as does the watercolor V. 822. *Afternoon at Naples* is based on the impression of Delacroix's *D e a t h   o f   Sardanapal* (Louvre) and *Women of Algiers in a Harem* (Louvre), as well as Manet's *Olympia* (Louvre). It belongs to the group of pictures with romantic-erotic subject matter. The story of Vollard as to the origin of the composition sounds rather spurious (Ambroise Vollard, *Paul Cézanne: His Life and Art,* New York, 1937, pp. 26-27). The paper is covered with several slight formulations of the movement of the two figures, and also shows some touches of young Paul Cézanne's scribblings (see remarks to Plate 38). The group to the left, although rendered with little anatomical correctness, shows a bold grasp of the expressive essentials of the two bodies.

6 MAN SURROUNDED BY RATS, c. 1875

Pencil. 124 x 217. Not in Venturi. Art Institute of Chicago.

John Rewald (ed.), *Paul Cézanne Carnet de Dessins,* Paris, 1951, I, 35, and II, 91; Carl O. Schniewind (ed.), *Paul Cézanne Sketch Book* (owned by the Art Institute of Chicago), New York, 1951, I, 30, and II, xxix verso.

Five of such sketch books have come in 1950 to the United States from Maurice Renou of Lyon, who had acquired them from the Cézanne family. One of the former owners numbered each page with a Roman numeral. The Chicago sketch book contains portraits, landscapes, numerous studies, and drawings by young Paul. Probably related to this drawing is the one reproduced in Adrien

Chappuis, *Dessins de Paul Cézanne*, Paris, 1938, Plate 19. In the upper part are crude sketches of two heads. As Carl Schniewind points out, the drawing recalls Delacroix as well as Daumier, without very direct relationship to any of the known works of these artists. The flowing hair, the fluttering shirt, and the open mouth give the impression of terrified flight, caused by the jumping rats. The scene recalls many representations of violence in the early and middle period of the artist. It is against this background of violence that the "classical" and objective style of the master emerges as a constant catharsis.

7 TWO WOMEN AT THE EDGE OF A RIVER, 1872-77

Pencil. 124 x 217. Not in Venturi. Art Institute of Chicago.
John Rewald (ed.), *Paul Cézanne Carnet de Dessins*, Paris, 1951, I, 35, and II, 87; Carl O. Schniewind (ed.), *Paul Cézanne Sketch Book* (owned by the Art Institute of Chicago), New York, 1951, I, 8, 31, and II, xxx verso.
Related to the crayon drawing (V. 1233) which adds a spatial setting with a boat and river, the drawing is interesting for its rather rare relaxed *joie de vivre* and for its rendering of everyday people. It places the drawing with those of Cézanne's Realist and Impressionist colleagues, especially Courbet (*Women at the Seine Resting*, Louvre) and Renoir. Rounded and undulating lines conform to the feminine fashions and forms.

8 OLYMPIA, 1875-77

Watercolor. 250 x 270. Venturi 882. Louis E. Stern, New York. (Photo Peter A. Juley & Son, New York.)
Ctlg. *Cézanne*, Fine Arts Associates, New York, 1952, No. 3 (repr.).
The watercolor, in which blue-gray tones prevail, belongs to a group of watercolors and paintings (V. 106, V. 225, V. 1206) which reflect the impression of Manet's *Olympia*. A painting by Cézanne of the same subject matter (V. 225) was exhibited at the first Impressionist show in 1874, lent by a friend of the Impressionist painters, Dr. Gachet in Auvers. Cézanne admired but also envied the elegant Manet and, accordingly, the watercolor, serious in its final intention, does not lack an element of mockery or satire. Cézanne, looking with deep concern at the nudes of Veronese, Tintoretto, Delacroix, and Manet, incorporated their echoes in his imaginary compositions. Awkward in drawing, developed in color, it can stand for the excitability and the still unresolved contradictions of his groping years.

9 WOMAN BATHER, 1873-82

Pencil. 206 x 130. Venturi 1250. Museum Boymans, Rotterdam. (Photo A. Frequin, Den Haag.)
Ctlg. *Paul Cézanne*, Den Haag, 1956, No. 111 (repr.); Ctlg. *Paul Cézanne*, Munich, 1956, No. 129 (repr.); Ctlg. *Paul Cézanne*, Kunsthaus, Zurich, 1956, No. 168.
The same figure is used in the compositions of *Four Bathing Women* (V. 384 and V. 1264), owned by the Boymans Museum in Rotterdam. The head is also used in the oil sketch V. 277, dated by Venturi 1873-77. The drawing might therefore be a few years earlier than Venturi's dating, 1879-82. The unquestionable awkwardness in the rendering of the female body is compensated by an expressive intensity which recalls the drawings of the early Kokoschka. The

position is probably taken from some picture by a sixteenth- or seventeenth-century master.

10 STUDY AFTER RUBENS' "LANDING OF MARIE DE MEDICI IN MARSEILLE" (Louvre), c. 1880

Pencil. 320 x 490. Venturi 1625. Mrs. W. Feilchenfeldt, Zurich. (Photo Walter Dräyer, Zurich.)
The drawing is derived from the lower section of the sixth picture of The Story of Marie de Medici. (A photograph of this Rubens composition was affixed to the walls of Cézanne's various lodgings [Joachim Gasquet, *Cézanne*, Paris, new edition, 1926, p. 74].) With the exception of the male figure to the left, who in the picture is blowing a shell, it is a quick yet precise rendition. It demonstrates the keen interest which Cézanne, even in his "classical" period, held for the work of Rubens. Venturi lists fourteen sketches after this artist. The understanding of the Flemish Baroque master was probably handed on to him through his favorite painter, Delacroix. In Rubens he could study the nude not in the dreaded academic model but in bodies which had become sinuous curves, plastic masses, chains of movement. They were stimuli for his great dream of a modern idyl with nudes.

11 BATHERS REPOSING, 1875-77

Watercolor and pen. 100 x 165. Venturi 899. Miss Gwendoline Davies. National Museum of Wales, Cardiff. (Photo Bernheim-Jeune, Paris.)
Fritz Novotny, *Cézanne*, New York (n.d.), Pl. 96; Ctlg. National Museum of Wales, *The Gwendoline Davies Bequest of Paintings, etc.*, Cardiff, 1952, No. 16.
This work belongs to the first bather group of watercolors V. 898-902, and is closely related to the paintings V. 273, 274, 276. The combination of watercolor and a sketchy pen line is unusual. In contrast to the light-colored oils of the same subject, this watercolor has an evening mood. The composition is conceived in large masses hinged on the shoulders of the downward-looking central figure. The highest light assembles around his head and in the cloud behind him. An element of Expressionist distortion removes the scene from the idyllic and the classical. One thinks of Cézanne's statement that "I wanted as in (Poussin's) *The Triumph of Flora* the curves of women married to the shoulders of hills" (Joachim Gasquet, *op. cit.*, p. 193).

12 THE DIVERS, 1879-82

Pencil. 180 x 270. Not in Venturi. Kraushaar Galleries. Arthur B. Davies. Los Angeles County Museum.
The present owner dates the drawing 1889-92, yet it belongs rather in the first group of studies for the bathers (V. 1256-1264) and especially to the watercolor V. 818. This is described by Venturi as *The Fall of Icarus* and dated too early (1865-70). Its Daumier-like line reminds one of the *Man Surrounded by Rats* (Plate 6). The drawing is interesting for its unusual subject. At that period, the sense for the dramatic is still strongly at work. Notice the correcting black lines, groping for anatomical expressiveness.

13 SKETCHES AROUND A BAROQUE ENGRAVING, probably 1878

Pencil. 320 x 240. Not in Venturi. Verso of Pl. 64. J. K. Thannhauser, New York.

Cézanne had made his drawing of L'Estaque (Plate 64) on the back of an engraving of an ornamental Baroque vase. Now he uses the remaining space for quick denotations of some frequently recurring ideas. There is the fisherman with hat, above it another male figure leaning on a table, in the right lower corner we find a fisherman again (or is it a man walking with a stick?), above it a female head copied from a vase, and sideways little Paul, sketched many times by his fond father. The drawing is related to the page from a sketch book (Plate 14) and to V. 1218 which is likewise done on the back of an engraving. As with many other artists, every available scrap of paper must serve for the incessant activity of the "thinking hand."

14 PAGE FROM A SKETCH BOOK, 1879-82

Pencil. 238 x 310. Venturi 1217. Museum Boymans, Rotterdam. (Photo A. Frequin, Den Haag.)

The drawing is important because it shows the artist incessantly observing or preparing ideas for compositions. It represents in the center a forward-stepping nude bather and next to it. a figure from Michelangelo's lost mural from the City Hall of Florence with "bathing soldiers" known to Cézanne from engravings. Two sketches of fishermen and a composition of an out-of-door scene refer to an Impressionist-classical idyl. Above the central bather, one notices a slight sketch for a bent

finger, and the remaining space is used for a likeness of his wife. Thus nature studies, copies from old masters, and imaginary compositions are combined on one page.

15 THE BATHER, 1878-82

Watercolor. 210 x 130. Venturi 905. Mr. and Mrs. Ira Haupt, New York.

Like Plate 16, this nude is rendered in the context of a nature setting. However, the counterpoint of the legs and arms indicates a "classical" source: in this instance, I believe, Michelangelo's *Battle of Pisa,* which is also reflected in the page from a sketch book (Plate 14). The artist did five known sketches after engravings of this mural. In two of them (V. 1225, 1298) he renders a figure with a very similar pose but seen from the back. This drawing represents a free paraphrase. Brush work and pencil line are free and fluid, and therefore give the classical motive its modern, nearly naturalistic feeling. In the words of Cézanne to Gasquet, "Imagine Poussin redone entirely upon nature, that is the classical as I understand it." (Bernard Dorival (ed.), *Cézanne par Ses Lettres et Ses Témoins,* Paris, 1948, p. 192)

16 THE BATHER, 1879-82

Pencil and watercolor. 215 x 150. Venturi 903. Wadsworth Athenaeum, Hartford.

Bernard Dorival, *Cézanne,* Paris, 1948, Pl. XVI; Georg Schmidt, *Watercolors by Paul Cézanne,* New York (n. d.), Pl. 5; Ctlg. *Paul Cézanne,* Art Institute of Chicago, Metropolitan Museum of Art, New York, 1952, No. 29 (repr.). The boy with a towel belongs to a painted composition of five figures (V. 390). There also exist two oil sketches (V. 393 and V. 394) and one nearly identical drawing (repr. Adrien Chappuis, *Dessins de Paul Cézanne*, Paris, 1938, Plate 33). Altogether there exist more than a hundred similar sketches in oil, watercolor, and drawing, executed throughout more than three decades. In sketches such as this the figures are still closer to reality than in the final stage of painting where they have abandoned any relation with a model; but even in a preparatory drawing the nude seems to be conceived from a contemplation of Delacroix, Poussin, and Michelangelo rather than from direct observation. The flowing outline is kept in suspended balance by the raised arm and the expansion of earth and sky. The isolated nude becomes a heroic silhouette in open space.

17 THE ENTOMBMENT AFTER CARAVAGGIO, 1879-85

Watercolor. 245 x 180. Venturi 869. Hans Hahnloser, Bern. (Photo Hans Schreiner, Munich.)
Ctlg. *Paul Cézanne*, Munich, 1956, No. 73. Ctlg. *Paul Cézanne*, Kunsthaus, Zurich, 1956, No. 208.
The free watercolor sketch, in blues, reds, and violets, was executed after an engraving, since Cézanne was never in the Vatican Pinacotheca. The artist occasionally drew from fashion plates or from the poor reproductions in Charles Le Blanc's *Histoire de Peintures de Toutes les Ecoles* (Paris, 1869), which he owned. The broadly brushed watercolor catches entirely the essentials of Caravaggio's Baroque composition. Nobody but Cézanne amongst his contemporaries would have shown an interest in this Baroque master.

18 MEDEA AFTER DELACROIX, 1879-82

Watercolor. 380 x 250. Venturi 867. Kunsthaus, Zurich. (Photo Walter Dräyer, Zurich.)
Julius Meier-Graefe, *Cézanne*, New York, 1937, Pl. XXX; Göran Schildt, *Paul Cézanne's Personligheit, etc.*, Helsigfors, 1947, Fig. 32; Lionello Venturi, *Paul Cézanne Water Colours*, Oxford, 1944, Fig. 8; Georg Schmidt, *Water-Colours by Paul Cézanne*, New York and Basle, (n. d.), Pl. 2; Ctlg. *Paul Cézanne*, Den Haag, 1956, No. 59 (repr.); Ctlg. *Paul Cézanne*, Munich, 1956, Pl. 72 (repr.); Ctlg. *Paul Cézanne*, Kunsthaus, Zurich, 1956, No. 96, Fig. 50
This watercolor is after Delacroix's *Medea* in the Museum at Lille. Cézanne was an ardent admirer of Delacroix, and actually owned a flower still life by this painter. He did a number of oils, watercolors, and drawings after the Romantic master, and as late as 1904 wrote to Emile Bernard: "I do not know whether my precarious health will still permit me to realize my dream of painting his (Delacroix's) apotheosis" (Emile Bernard, *Souvenirs sur Paul Cézanne*, Paris, 1912, p. 71). As in his other studies, it is the violence and passion expressed in half modern and half "Baroque" forms that stirred Cézanne. While Delacroix is responsible for the tragic fury of the picture, Cézanne raised its possibilities far beyond the original work. The merely illustrative elements have been translated into a consistent rhythmical organization as can be seen by a comparison with the background in Delacroix's picture. He uses in general green-blue and light brown washes, but the red drapery behind the struggling child on the left introduces a coloristic symbol of the

40

imminent bloodshed. As in Van Gogh's sketches after Delacroix, the "Expressionistic" qualities are enhanced beyond the style of Delacroix.

19 AMOR AFTER PUGET'S STATUE IN THE LOUVRE, 1888-95

Pencil. 480 x 315. Venturi 1457. Brooklyn Museum.
Ctlg. *Paul Cézanne,* San Francisco Museum of Art, 1937, No. 66; Ctlg. *Paul Cézanne,* Art Institute of Chicago, Metropolitan Museum of Art, New York, 1952, No. 92 (repr.).
Venturi lists nine drawings, four watercolors, and five oils of the same subject. Thus, it surpasses in frequency the studies after Houdon's *L'Ecorché* (see Plate 25), another favorite subject of the artist. Cézanne owned casts of these two works and therefore could use them as models, which, unlike living ones, would neither tire nor change. In Puget he experienced the Baroque, or, as he said to Gasquet, "There is a southwind (mistral) in Puget. He uses wandering shadows as his contemporaries used underpaint" (Joachim Gasquet, *op cit.,* p. 191). It seems as if the artist felt the presence of these works of art a constant challenge, of which he freed himself in drawing them from every possible angle. The drawing emphasizes the rippling contour, which contains the chubby body of a child. The diagonal thrust of the shoulder is taken up in the oil painting (V. 706) by the diagonally placed canvases set up behind the still life. A peculiar feature of the pose reverberates in the entire composition.

20 BATHERS, 1882-94

Watercolor. 145 x 200. Venturi 902. Mr.

and Mrs. Walter Annenberg, Wynnewood, Pennsylvania.
Vollard has dated the watercolor 1882, but Venturi rightly points out that the style is later. Related to V. 901 and 1114. The drawing was first owned by Renoir. The watercolor is drawn with the brush over pencil with touches of green, blue, and yellow. The grouping recalls the lithograph *Bathing Men* (V. 1156).

21 NUDE AFTER SIGNORELLI, 1882-90

Black crayon. 182 x 116. Not in Venturi. Mr. and Mrs. Ira Haupt, New York.
John Rewald (ed.), *Paul Cézanne Carnet de Dessins,* Paris, 1951, I, 28, and II, No. 115 (repr.). From a sketch book owned by Mr and Mrs. Haupt, p. 35 verso.
We know from Vollard (and Gasquet) that Cézanne had a reproduction after Signorelli's *The Living Bearing the Dead* (Orvieto Cathedral) on his wall. Emile Bernard also tells us that Cézanne paid great attention to this artist, "but more for his style than for his muscles" (*Souvenirs sur Paul Cézanne,* p. 47).
In this instance the drawing is a rather precise copy of a figure study today in the Louvre (repr. Kenneth Clark, *The Nude,* New York, 1956, p. 200). Signorelli's style has been slightly altered in the direction of an elongated mannerism. The artist collected such nudes in which he wanted to fuse the classical configuration of idealized figures with atmospheric "modern" painting. Since he drew but rarely from models, he was constantly on the lookout for expressive poses in other artist's paintings.

22 ST. GEORGE, 1885-95

Pencil with traces of watercolor. 311 x 213. Venturi 1080. After a plaster cast of Donatello's statue at Or' San Michele in Florence in the Trocadéro. Albertina, Vienna.

Ctlg. *Paul Cézanne,* San Francisco Museum of Art, 1937, No. 65 (repr.) ; John Rewald, *Cézanne et Zola,* Paris, 1936, No. 67.

One of the hundreds of drawings which the artist executed in the Louvre (today in the Trocadéro) with its excellent collection of casts. Interestingly enough, there are many more drawings after sculptures than after paintings. See Plates 19, 25, and 44.

The spread-legged stance of the statue is neglected in favor of the emphatic rendering of the shoulder and arm section. The proportions are, as frequently in this period, elongated. Bands of color indicate the statue's location in a niche.

23 HARLEQUIN, 1888

Pencil. 470 x 301. Venturi 1486. Art Institute of Chicago.

Julius Meier-Graefe, *Cézanne,* Pl. 76; Göran Schildt, *Paul Cézanne's Personligheit, etc.,* Fig. 10; Ctlg. *Paul Cézanne,* Art Institute of Chicago, Metropolitan Museum of Art, New York, 1952, No. 72 (repr.) .

This is a preparatory drawing for the painting *Mardi Gras* (V. 552), and for the watercolor V. 1079. The son of the artist is the model. The picture was painted in the artist's studio in Paris in 1888. A study of the head is to be found in Plate 41. As in the figures of the "Mannerists" of the sixteenth century, the body becomes elongated, the head very small. An expressive dematerialization is the result. This char-

acter is further enhanced by the calm of the features. With this picture, the keen and exploratory work of the latest phase marks its beginning.

24 STUDY OF A NUDE FIGURE, c. 1885-95

Pencil with touches of watercolor. 635 x 490. Not in Venturi. Ambroise Vollard. Pierre F. Nesi. J. K. Thannhauser. Fogg Museum of Art, Harvard University, Cambridge, Massachusetts.

Ctlg. *Golden Gate International Exhibition,* San Francisco, 1940, No. 415; Fogg Museum of Art, Harvard University, *Annual Report,* 1954-55, p. 16 (repr.) .

The model—according to the San Francisco catalogue—was Michelangelo di Rosa, his favorite youthful sitter (see Plate 45) . This drawing is related to the drawing of St. George after Donatello (see Plate 22) with its elongated body, small head, and relatively continuous delineation. The studio props indicate that it seems to be done from a live model. This is very unusual in the late period of the artist, when he relied mostly on his memory and was afraid, furthermore, of small-town talk. Yet even when using a live model, he renders the "inner form" so powerfully that the proportions take on an entirely personal character. As so often in his drawings, a few lines and touches in the background provide the figure with an architectural accompaniment.

25 STUDY AFTER HOUDON'S "L'ECORCHE," 1888-95

Pencil. 275x210. Venturi 1452. Verso of V. 1115. Metropolitan Museum of Art, New York (on loan to the Museum of

Modern Art, New York).

Ctlg. *Masterpieces of 19th and 20th Century French Drawings*, Detroit Institute of Arts, 1941, No. 1; Ctlg. *Modern Drawings*, Museum of Modern Art, New York, 1944; John Rewald, *Paul Cézanne*, New York, 1948, Fig. 95; Charles Slatkin and Regina Schoolman, *Six Centuries of French Master Drawings in America*, New York, 1950, Pl. 107.

Drawn after the cast in the Ecole des Beaux Arts in Paris. Cézanne was intrigued by the baring of the bone structure and the muscular anatomy in this statue, which satisfied his curiosity for the underlying structure of appearances. As in some drawings of late still lifes, he applies an undulating rhythm to the plastic forms. These forms are expressively elongated, the inner and outer contours correspond to each other, and a horizontal and diagonal line in the background create a module for distances and directions. Cézanne himself owned the cast of another flayed man (*L'ecorché*) of whom there are not less than nine sketches in the Chicago sketch book (see *Paul Cézanne's Sketch Book* [owned by the Art Institute of Chicago], New York, 1951, p. 27, No. XI).

PORTRAITS

26 HEAD AND HAND STUDIES OF THE PAINTER ACHILLE EMPERAIRE, 1867-69

Charcoal on buff paper. 315 x 490. Venturi 1193. David Lederer. Elvira B. Reilly, New York.

Julius Meier-Graefe, *Cézanne und Sein Kreis*, Munich, 1922, p. 90; J. B. Neumann (ed.), *Art Lover Library*, Gallerie Günther Franke, Munich and New York, III, 22; Ctlg. *Paul Cézanne*, Art Institute of Chicago, Metropolitan Museum of Art, New York, 1952 No. 9 (repr.).

This head as well as Plate 4 are studies for the painting *The Autopsy* (V. 105). The painter-friend from Aix served as a model. Adrien Chappuis, *Dessins de Cézanne* (1957, No. 3), does not believe that this is the same head as in our No. 4. We cannot follow him in this point According to Joachim Gasquet (*Cézanne*, pp. 38-39) Emperaire was "a dwarf, but with a magnificent cavalier's head, like a Van Dyck, nerves of steel, an iron pride in a deformed body, a flame of genius on a warped hearth, a mixture of Don Quixote and Prometheus." Emile Bernard, in his *Souvenirs sur Paul Cézanne*, also recalls the master's description of his friend (pp. 49-50). The drawing technique is robust but catches the essentials of the features and hands in an undulating stroke which is consistent throughout. Cézanne has taken a great step beyond the academic nudes.

27 CEZANNE'S FATHER READING THE NEWSPAPER, 1868-70

Pencil. 207 x 125. Venturi 1403. Robert von Hirsch, Basle.

John Rewald, *Cézanne et Zola*, Paris, 1936, No. 48; John Rewald, *Paul Cézanne*, New York, 1948, p. 112.

From the third sketch book, today almost in its entirety in the Kunstmuseum, Basle. (Dated by Rewald about 1880, which, in my opinion, is much too late.) Related to the painting of the same subject matter (V. 91), yet not a preparatory drawing for it. This early drawing shows the typical undulating "Baroque" line of the artist which stands in so strange a contrast to the "classical" spirit of his later compositions. It probably owes some of its character to Daumier and Delacroix. It is quite different from the later, more geometrically conceived drawing of his father (Plate 40).

This drawing catches with nicety the enclosure of the figure by the armchair, the expressive cap with its light-reflecting visor and the relaxed position of the crossed legs. It is from the spirit of these early drawings that we understand why old Cézanne was much impressed by the drawings of Forain.

28 PORTRAIT OF CAMILLE PISSARRO, c. 1873

Pencil. 100 x 80. Not in Venturi. Camille Pissarro. Lucien Pissarro. Leicester Gallery. Sir Hugh Walpole. F. Sprinzels. Mr. and Mrs. John Rewald.
John Rewald, *Cézanne, Sa Vie, Son Oeuvre, etc.,* Paris, 1939, No. 34; John Rewald (ed.), *Camille Pissarros Letters to His Son Lucien,* London and New York, 1943, No. 49; Ctlg. *Cézanne,* Wildenstein and Co., New York, 1947, No. 87 (repr.); John Rewald, *Paul Cézanne,* New York, 1948, Fig. 44; John Rewald, *The Ordeal of Paul Cézanne,* London, 1950, Fig. 33.
See also Plates 29 and 30. This small sketch, without claim to artistic importance, gives us a welcome glimpse of the patriarchal head of the Impressionist painter of whom Cézanne spoke and wrote in reverence. An unfailing friend, ever encouraging in spite of his own financial misery, a guide toward the ethical basis of an uncompromisingly naturalistic art—this is the reason why Cézanne called him "the humble and colossal Pissarro."

29 PORTRAIT OF PISSARRO, 1872-76

Pencil. 195 x 113. Venturi 1235. Musée du Louvre, Paris.
John Rewald (ed.), *Correspondance de Paul Cézanne,* Paris, 1937, No. 34; Ctlg. *Homage to Paul Cézanne,* Wildenstein and Co., London, 1939, No. 77; Fritz Novotny, *Cézanne,* Vienna and New York, (n.d.), No. 119; John Rewald, *Paul Cézanne,* New York, 1948, Fig. 42.
This direct sketch shows the painter Camille Pissarro, ready to walk with stick and knapsack to his "motive." The broad-brimmed hat casts a shadow over the bearded features of the admired friend. The drawing is made after a photograph which shows Pissarro and Cézanne in front of a garden wall (repr. John Rewald, *Cézanne et Zola,* Paris, 1936, Fig. 32). The free line, the atmospheric shadows, bespeak the naturalistic tendencies of this period. The drawing is under Pissarro's influence, yet the pose, especially in its relation to the background, introduces a slightly geometrical element, completely absent in the work of the other Impressionists.

30 CAMILLE PISSARRO SKETCHING. MADAME CEZANNE. PEASANT WOMAN, c. 1881

Pencil. 217 x 126. Mr. and Mrs. Leigh B. Block, Chicago.
John Rewald (ed.), *Paul Cézanne Carnet de Dessins,* Paris, 1951, I, 51, and II, No. 15 (repr.). From a sketch book owned by Mr. and Mrs. Block, p. II .
The sketch book in which these drawings appeared was used by Cézanne between 1875 and 1885. We have chosen this sheet for its autobiographical character. In 1881, Cézanne worked with Pissarro in Pontoise, visited with Zola in Médan, or lived with his family in

Paris. The simple sketch speaks of the people whom he loved and trusted.

31 SELF PORTRAIT, 1875-77

Pencil. 217 x 124. Not in Venturi. Art Institute of Chicago.
John Rewald (ed.), *Paul Cézanne Carnet de Dessins,* Paris, 1951, I, 34, and II, 4; Carl O. Schniewind (ed.), *Paul Cézanne Sketch Book* (owned by the Art Institute of Chicago), New York, 1951, I, 12, 29, and II, xxii.
This is the earliest of five self portraits in this sketch book. The artist, nearly bald at thirty-five, presented himself in the sober mood of a provincial citizen. The drawing lacks the spirituality which appears in Plate 33. It is unusual exactly for this element of impersonal detachment.

32 SELF PORTRAIT, 1880-82

Pencil. 217 x 124. Not in Venturi. Art Institute of Chicago.
John Rewald (ed.), *Paul Cézanne Carnet de Dessins,* Paris, 1951, I No. 33, and II, No. 2; Carl O. Schniewind (ed.), *Paul Cézanne Sketch Book* (owned by the Art Institute of Chicago), New York, 1951, I, 13, 26, and II, vii verso.
The beard is larger in comparison with Plate 31, and enhances the physical and spiritual importance of the head. The lines of the outer circumscription as well as the inner ones are more calligraphic and establish a rhythm of mass and light. The eyes have lost their previous timid expression, and look with enduring strength at the outer world. The actual likeness has yielded to an all-absorbing confrontation with the self.

33 SELF PORTRAIT, 1885-86

Pencil. 217 x 124. Not in Venturi. Art Institute of Chicago.
John Rewald (ed.), *Paul Cézanne Carnet de Dessins,* Paris, 1951, I, 36, and II, 1; Carl O. Schniewind (ed.), *Paul Cézanne Sketch Book* (owned by the Art Institute of Chicago), New York, 1951, I, 13, 32, and II, xxxvii.
This portrait appears as the one with the greatest inner and outer likeness. The glance is weary, the mouth joyless. One feels a tremendous burden weighing upon the artist, but also the power of endurance. One eye is larger and more distinctly rendered than the other. While Plate 32 is unusually regular and symmetrical, this portrait, with the head slightly bent forward, catches the actual moment of perception.

34 SELF PORTRAIT, c. 1895

Pencil. 240 x 150. Venturi 1304. Adrien Chappuis, Tresserve (Savoie, France). Adrien Chappuis, *Dessins de Paul Cézanne,* Paris, 1938, Pl. 47. From the third Chappuis sketch book, Pl. X, loose sheet.
The latest of the drawn self portraits. An element of spiritual intensification lends deep seriousness to this head— a tormented sage with a distant resemblance to the features of Dostoevsky.

35 PORTRAIT OF MADAME CEZANNE, 1880-85

Pencil. 280 x 210. Not in Venturi. O. T. Falk. Mrs. E. F. Hutton, New York. (Photo Knoedler Galleries, New York.)
Ctlg. *Cézanne,* Fine Arts Associates, New York, 1952, No. 6 (repr.).
Of the many drawn likenesses of the

artist's wife, we have chosen this portrait because of its rare gentleness, enhanced by the luminous quality of the lightly used pencil. There are a few correcting lines in the nose and hair. The diagonal position of the figure comes closest to the oil painting V. 521, which, however, has lost the relaxed expression. When the drawing is turned at right angles, one sees the study for a lady's waist and bustle.

36 MADAME CEZANNE, c. 1890

Pencil. 240 x 150. Venturi 1303. Adrien Chappuis, Tresserve (Savoie, France). Adrien Chappuis, *Dessins de Paul Cézanne*, Paris, 1938, Pl. 32. From the third Chappuis sketch book, Pl. VII.

In this portrait the wife of the artist is shown at the same age and in the same dress as in the painting *Madame Cézanne in the Conservatory* (V. 569). Even the diagonal position of the head is identical. It is also related to the drawing in Museum Boymans, Rotterdam (V. 1467) (see Plate 37). As in many of Cézanne's paintings, the eyes are rendered as black circles without indication of the pupils. Nevertheless, the impression is one of attentiveness, so different from the usual passive expression of his models. The pure oval of the head, together with the rectangular lines to the right, enhance the feeling of a perfectly ordered impression. There seems to be a pervasive element of sympathy with the sitter.

37 MADAME CEZANNE, 1883-86

Pencil. 480 x 320. Venturi 1467. Museum Boymans, Rotterdam. (Photo A. Frequin, Den Haag.)
P. Cassirer, *Franssche Meesters uit de XIXe*, Amsterdam, 1938, No. 21; *Teekeningen van Franssche Meesters*, Stedelijk Museum, Amsterdam, 1946, No. 14; *Les Dessins Français de Fouquet à Cézanne*, Brussels, Rotterdam, and Paris, 1949-50, No. 206, Pl. 91; *Dessins du Musée Boymans*, Bibliothèque Nationale, Paris, 1952, No. 141; Ctlg. *Paul Cézanne*, Art Institute of Chicago, Metropolitan Museum of Art, New York, 1952, No. 45 (repr.); *French Drawings: Masterpieces from Seven Centuries*, Chicago, etc., 1955-56, No. 156, Pl. 40.

Madame Cézanne, in her finery with high-buttoned dress and a draped hat, leaning against the back of a chair, her mouth compressed, her eyes intent—what a naturalistic likeness! And yet the homogeneous element of the curvature in dress, cheek, and hat lend a unified rhythmical quality to the drawing. The duplication of the silhouette in the shadow and the slanting diagonal of the position likewise enhance the formal intensity of the drawing. But, most of all, how much of Cézanne's spirit has entered into the concentrated immobility of his sitter.

38 PORTRAIT OF THE ARTIST'S SON, 1880-82

Black pencil. 275 x 230. Detail from a sheet of sketches. Not in Venturi. Albertina, Vienna (inv. 24087).
John Rewald (ed.), *Correspondance de Paul Cézanne*, Pl. 25; John Rewald, *Paul Cézanne*, New York, 1948, p. 99.

See also Plate 39. The artist's son Paul, born in 1872, is a favorite subject of Cézanne. He not only renders him in various poses and activities, but he also permits him to share the pages of his sketch books, of which we have frequent and amusing traces (see Carl O.

Schniewind [ed.], *Paul Cézanne Sketch Book* [owned by the Art Institute of Chicago], New York, 1951.

39 THE ARTIST'S SON PAUL, 1880-82

Pencil. 215 x 126. Venturi 1284. Adrien Chappuis, Tresserve (Savoie, France). John Rewald (ed.), *Correspondance de Paul Cézanne*, No. 25; Adrien Chappuis, *Dessins de Paul Cézanne,* Paris, 1938, Pl. 23. From the second Chappuis sketch book, Pl. X verso.
See also Plate 38. Paul seems to be about ten years of age in this drawing. The technique is naturalistic, the expression spontaneous. As in some drawings of Cézanne's wife, a tender approval of the object of his observation softens the expression.

40 THE FATHER OF THE ARTIST, 1880-86

Pencil. 217 x 124. Not in Venturi. Art Institute of Chicago.
John Rewald (ed.), *Paul Cézanne Carnet de Dessins,* Paris, 1951, I, 35, and II, 10; Carl O. Schniewind (ed.), *Paul Cézanne Sketch Book* (owned by the Art Institute of Chicago), New York, 1951, I, 14, 30, and II, xxix.
See also Plate 27. One of three sketches of Cézanne's father who is known to us especially from the early paintings while reading a newspaper (V. 25, 91, 227). The eyes remain invisible, increasing the feeling of block-like immobility which the artist has further emphasized in the cubic superimposition of the square face, the visor of the cap and its angular top. Form and expression are developed in the closest and simplest relationship. The fact that

the father is sleeping may be concluded from a similar sketch showing him with his eyes closed (repr. *Carnet de Dessins,* Plate II).

41 STUDY FOR THE HARLEQUIN IN "MARDI GRAS," 1888

Pencil. 190 x 255. Venturi 1622. Robert von Hirsch, Basle.
See remarks to Plate 23. As opposed to the finished picture (V. 552), the likeness of the head to the model, young Paul Cézanne, is still fully preserved. However, the spirit of the adolescent has changed into one of severe scrutiny, the personality of the artist already fusing with that of his model. Sharp, deeply black lines establish the rhythm of the contour in the hat and along the cheek over the first softer drawing. The central part of the face is slightly sketched a second time to the right.

42 PORTRAIT OF A PEASANT, 1890-92

Black chalk. 271 x 192. Venturi 1587 (verso: landscape). Kupferstichkabinett der Offentlichen Kunstsammlung, Basle (inv. 1934. 204).
Related to the oil studies, V. 561, 563, and 565, done in relationship with the standing peasant behind the card players in the paintings, V. 559 and 560. The stronger condensing lines have been drawn over the first light sketch.

43 THE CARD PLAYER, 1890-92

Pencil with traces of watercolor. 484 x 362. Venturi 1086. Museum of Art, Rhode Island School of Design, Providence.

47

Hans Tietze, *European Master Drawings in the United States*, New York, 1947, No. 151; Agnes Mongan, *One Hundred Master Drawings*, Cambridge, 1949, p. 194; Paul J. Sachs, *Modern Prints and Drawings*, New York, 1954, Pl. 34; Kurt Badt, *Die Kunst Cézannes*, Munich, 1956, Fig. 16.

Study for the picture of one of the "Card Players" in the Barnes Foundation at Merion, Pennsylvania (V. 560) and its second version in the Stephen Clarke Collection in New York (V. 559). Besides dozens of oil sketches, there exist watercolors and drawings in which the artist prepared this figure composition, of central importance in his work. The drawing is first laid in with pencil and then implemented in the upper parts by a few brush strokes of violet. Notice how in the hat and in the silhouette of the frock the lines have undergone a slightly angular simplification aiming at the larger context of the composition. In this sense, the rectilinear forms of the table are also of importance. Cézanne is much less concerned with the psychological expression of the card player than he is absorbed by the massive weightiness of his model, to whom he lends a lasting solidity.

44 HEAD OF RICHELIEU, 1890-95

Pencil and charcoal. 205 x 114. Venturi 1364. After the bust by Bernini in the Louvre. Kupferstichkabinett der Offentlichen Kunstsammlung, Basle (inv. 1935.113).
Fritz Novotny, *Cézanne,* (n. d.), No. 126. From the second Basle sketch book, p. v.

The fact that Cézanne did a considerable number of heads after sculptures in the Louvre indicates that the artist was not only concerned with problems of form, but wanted as well to grasp the "spirit" of the objects he studied. This drawing shows keen understanding of the physiognomical elements and of their Baroque character. The proportions are slightly elongated, and owing to omissions and shadow accents, the head seems to be transformed from a sculpture into a painting.

45 BOY WITH THE RED VEST, 1890-95

Watercolor. 460 x 300. Venturi 1094. Mrs. W. Feilchenfeldt, Zurich.
Ctlg. *Cézanne,* Wildenstein and Co., New York, 1947, No. 78 (repr.); Georg Schmidt, *Watercolours by Paul Cézanne,* No. 31, Art Institute of Chicago, Metropolitan Museum of Art, New York, 1952, No. 74 (repr.); Ctlg. *Paul Cézanne,* Kunsthaus, Zurich, 1956, No. 110, Fig. 51; Ctlg. *Paul Cézanne,* Munich, 1956, No. 85 (repr.); Ctlg. *Paul Cézanne,* Den Haag, 1956, No. 70 (repr.); Ctlg. *Cézanne,* Cologne, 1957, No. 38 (repr.).

The model, an Italian boy, Michelangelo Di Rosa, sat for four paintings (V. 680-683) and this watercolor, all of them done in the same period. The most naturalistic one (V. 680), rendering the boy in profile, has recently been acquired by the Museum of Modern Art in New York. The long-haired model and the red vest have inspired Cézanne to do some of the grandest portraits of the nineteenth century.

This watercolor is unusually loose in the free flow of agitated lines, drawn exclusively with the brush, and in the nearly ferocious spotting of the surface with blue-green tints. The red tones of the vest, overlaid with some brown and blue, are more transparent than the photograph can show. Owing to the saddle seat and the large hands, in combination with the violent execution, the watercolor contains an element of repressed excitement which contrasts with the stillness of the paintings.

46 PORTRAIT OF VOLLARD, 1899

Pencil. 430 x 330. Venturi 1480. Private collection, Paris. Frederick B. Deknatel, Cambridge, Massachusetts.
Vollard, the dealer of Cézanne and of many important contemporaries, reproduced this drawing in his Cézanne book (Paris, 1915) and dated it 1899. In the same book he gives a lively, although probably exaggerated account of the innumerable portrait sessions from which his austere oil portrait (V. 696) emerged. In comparison with it, the drawing is loose and naturalistic, indicating how a phase of verisimilitude preceded a later one of formal condensation. The style is unusually vaporous for Cézanne, and tends toward a crayon technique. Undulating lines laid over the first drawing enforce unity. In the oil they have yielded to a rigid pyramidal design.

47 SEATED PEASANT, 1900-04

Watercolor. 450 x 300. Venturi 1089. Kunsthaus, Zurich.
Ctlg. *Paul Cézanne*, Den Haag, 1956, No. 83 (repr.); Ctlg. *Paul Cézanne*, Munich, 1956, No. 106 (repr.); Ctlg. *Paul Cézanne*, Kunsthaus, Zurich, 1956, No. 134, Fig. 62.
Study for the oil, V. 713, which shows the model against a patterned wallpaper. As in the watercolor *Boy with the Red Vest* (Plate 45), the closeness

of the image and a symmetrical position lend the scene its nearly hieratic monumentality. The old peasant belongs in the same group of senescent people whom the artist liked to represent during the last years of his life. Their immobile pose on which often a warm sun casts its light, their simple relationship to nature, evoke in the artist a feeling of brotherly sympathy. The colors in this as in the other late figure studies are expressively heightened. The model is entirely drawn with the brush, the silhouette and the definition of local color being one.

48 THE GARDENER VALLIER, 1900-06

Watercolor. 475 x 310. Venturi 1092. Siegfried Kramarsky, New York.
Ctlg. *Paul Cézanne*, Art Institute of Chicago, Metropolitan Museum of Art, New York, 1952, No. 120 (repr.); Ctlg. *Paul Cézanne*, Den Haag, 1956, No. 88 (repr.); Ctlg *Cézanne's Watercolors*, Fine Arts Associates, New York, 1956, No. 24 (repr.); Ctlg. *Paul Cézanne*, Kunsthaus, Zurich, 1956, No. 139, Fig. 63; Ctlg. *Cézanne*, Aix-en-Provence, 1956, No. 85.
There exist two oil sketches in the same position (V. 15 and V. 1524), one other watercolor (repr. Lionello Venturi, *Paul Cézanne Watercolours*, Plate 29), and two watercolors of Vallier seen in profile (V. 1102).
The style of Cézanne's old age is apparent in the hurrying looseness of the pencil lines and the light touch of the coloring brush. Trees form on both sides an enclosure that enriches and denaturalizes the silhouette. Flowing around the old man is sunlight, taking away something of the weight of age and of matter.

STILL LIFES

49 THE GREEN JAR, 1885-95

Watercolor. 195 x 232. Venturi 1138.
Musée du Louvre, Paris.
George Waldemar (ed.), *Aquarelles de Paul Cézanne,* Paris (n.d.), color plate.
The painter had a distinct liking for pottery with a warm moss-green glaze. Various shapes of this type appear in his still lifes. The watercolor is executed to the point of finality. In monumental equilibrium the globular form of the jar is set against a blue-gray background which—owing to the slanting line to the right—seems to recede diagonally. By casting a darker green shadow against the background, the jar projects its rotund form upon the flat background. This is one of the few watercolors in which the color modulation follows meticulously the drawn silhouette of the vessel.

50 CANDLE HOLDER AND DIVERSE OBJECTS, 1894-1900

Black chalk. 100 x 177. Venturi 1419. Kupferstichkabinett der Offentlichen Kunstsammlung, Basle (inv. 1935.185). From the third Basle sketch book, p. xvii.
The coordination of circular and vertical forms is related to certain late still lifes with their combination of conically shaped objects placed close together. See especially the watercolor with bottles, pots, and alcohol stove, Plate 60 (V. 1541).

51 UNMADE BED, after 1880

Pencil. 273 x 210. Venturi 1317. Adrien

Chappuis. Private collection, France. Adrien Chappuis, *Dessins de Paul Cézanne,* Paris, 1938, Pl. 41; Ctlg. *Homage to Paul Cézanne,* Wildenstein and Co., London, 1939, No. 83. From the fourth Chappuis sketch book, Pl. LXV.
In his later years Cézanne liked to sketch objects from his daily life, extracting from them both a monumental quality and an agitated expressiveness. The *Lit Défait (Unmade Bed),* of which there exists also a watercolor (V. 1316, LII), gains its intensive effect from a close-up which focuses the eye on the bizarre forms of the pillows contrasted with the geometrical volutes of the metal bed. The fact that only the upper part of the bed is visible enhances the largeness of the design.

52 ROCOCO CLOCK, AFTER 1885

Black pencil. 212 x 132. Venturi 1330. Verso of V. 1329, sketch after the statue of the so-called *Dying Seneca* in the Louvre. Kupferstichkabinett der Offentlichen Kunstsammlung, Basle (inv. 1935.141 verso).
From the first Basle sketch book, p vi verso.
We have chosen this drawing because it shows the transformation of an object into a consistent linear rhythm. The Rococo design is condensed to its basic curvilinear movement. From childhood, Cézanne had been exposed to the Baroque and Rococo in his native surroundings, and had deeply absorbed their curved and fluent lines. He also painted a Rococo vase (V. 222) and various Baroque sculptures (see Plates 19, 25, and 44).

53 ORNAMENT IN THE STYLE OF LOUIS XIV, after 1885

Pencil. 240 x 150. Venturi 1304. Adrien Chappuis, Tresserve (Savoie, France). Adrien Chappuis, *Dessins de Paul Cézanne,* Paris, 1938, Pl. 48. From the third Chappuis sketch book, p. xii verso.

The sketch books owned by Chappuis were used by the artist between 1879 and 1895, as may be concluded from some written denotations. If the drawing of the apples (Plate 59) explored a simple, circular rhythm, here the artist extracts rhythmical order from a Baroque (or Rococo) design. The undulating curves are applied in bilateral symmetry and with a completely even pressure of the drawing hand. The drawing of a Rococo clock from the Basle sketch book (Plate 52) belongs in the same context. In these drawings the artist is applying his search for the underlying geometry of nature to the higher organism of an expressive Baroque style. The synthesis of the two is unique in the nineteenth century.

54 THREE PEARS, 1888

Watercolor. 230 x 310. Venturi 1136. Henry Pearlman, New York.
Ctlg. *Cézanne's Watercolors,* Fine Arts Associates, New York, 1956, No. 10 (repr.).
This watercolor is not so much a preparatory study as a completely finished composition in its own right. In design and color it tends more toward an expressive decoration than toward a naturalistic portrayal. Unbroken curves keep the design of plate and fruit in constant motion. Two of the pears approach each other's silhouettes at the middle axis, while a third one unites

them by its arc. A Rococo spray in the wallpaper paraphrases the motive. In color, too, the light touch of yellow and green in the fruits, of violet in the wallpaper, departs from the natural coloration of the objects. The watercolor was once owned by Edgar Degas who was probably attracted by its "artificial" color, paralleling that of his late pastels.

55 STILL LIFE WITH EGGPLANT, POMEGRANATES, A SUGAR BOWL, AND A CARAFE ON A TABLE, 1895-1905

Watercolor. 305 x 470. Venturi 1145. Mr. and Mrs. Walter Annenberg, Wynnewood, Pennsylvania.
The choice and crowded juxtaposition of the objects is unusual among the still lifes. The selection was apparently prompted by the artist's wish to combine a number of rounded bodies; therefore we find the eggplant in combination with the bulbous pieces of china and glass. The diagonal arrangement enhances the feeling of pressure. The color scheme aims at a unity of blue-green tones.

56 STILL LIFE WITH SOUP BOWL AND BRONZE GOBLET, c. 1890

Watercolor. Measurements unknown. Venturi 848. Bernheim-Jeune. George Bernheim. Matzukata, Tokyo. (Photo Bernheim-Jeune, Paris.)
After the painting V. 200, but executed many years later. The same arrangement also appears in the extremely strange *Preparation for a Banquet* (V. 586). We have chosen this still life for its anti-classical Baroque line, which is

most unusual in the late period. It was probably the bronze goblet which aroused emotions of Oriental sumptuousness. The usually static composition is dissolved, and an undulating rhythm transforms the objects into a flowing and nearly hallucinatory pattern. That Cézanne must have connected far-reaching associations with this composition is evident from the fact that in V. 586 he surrounded it with nude figures carrying classical containers and enclosed it in a tent.

57 COAT OVER A CHAIR, 1890-1900

Watercolor and pencil. 455 x 285. Venturi 1125. Mrs. W. Feilchenfeldt, Zurich. (Photo Walter Dräyer, Zurich.) Maurice Raynal, *Cézanne*, Paris, 1936, p. 138 (repr.); Bernard Dorival, *Cézanne*, Pl. XVIII, No. 1, text p. 181; Ctlg. *Paul Cézanne*, Kunsthaus, Zurich, 1956, No. 119, Fig. 57.

It is a peculiar feature of Cézanne's art that tablecloths and other textiles are molded as if they were solid forms and thus take part as objects in the composition. They look as if they were cut from sheet metal; the folds and indentations are as mountainous and mysterious as the "landscape" of pillows to the eyes of a child. Here a maximum of drama is extracted from the old coat draped over a chair. The body-forms of its wearer seem still contained in it. The rich play of flowing, heavy curves lend a simple majesty to an everyday object. One is reminded of Van Gogh's *Chair with Pipe* (Tate Gallery, London) in which likewise the commonplace has become the carrier of emotions expressed in terms of simplified monumentality.

58 APPLES AND INK BOTTLE, 1895-1900

Watercolor. 310 x 450. Not in Venturi. Mrs. Lilly Wulf. Fine Arts Associates. Mr. and Mrs. Paul Hirschland, New York.
John Rewald (ed.), *Cézanne: Ten Watercolors*, New York, 1947 (in color); Ctlg. *Paul Cézanne*, Art Institute of Chicago, Metropolitan Museum of Art, New York, 1952, No. 89 (repr.); Ctlg. *Cézanne*, Fine Arts Associates, New York, 1956, No. 16.

The watercolor holds a midway position between the drawing of six apples (Plate 59) and the still life with alcohol stove (Plate 60), between the simplest units of circular forms and the most complex configuration of many objects placed closely together. The pen introduces a diagonal, frequent in late designs, which relates to half of a segmental arch in the background. Originally a flask might have been intended on the right side, as the silhouette, repeated four times, indicates. Different from the "slipping" perspective of so many of his painted still lifes, the objects are rendered here on a broad and static table surface, a study in equilibrium of form, of harmony in color. The sparing use of color shows blue in the ink bottle, red and yellow in the fruits, while the background is rendered in tan, green, and blue.

59 SIX APPLES, 1895-1900

Pencil. 210 x 273. Venturi 1316. Adrien Chappuis, Tresserve (Savoie, France). Ctlg. *Paul Cézanne*, San Francisco Museum of Art, 1937, No. 70 (repr., wrong measurements); Adrien Chappuis, *Dessins de Paul Cézanne*, Paris,

1938, Pl. 44. From the fourth Chappuis sketch book, p. xxviii.

This drawing is related to the watercolor V. 1132 which shows in addition a wine glass and another apple to the right. It is a study in equilibrium, in which the perfect circles of the fruit combined with the oval of the platter create a design of suspended motion. One may compare it with the watercolor V. 854 from about 1875, the naturalistic version of the same subject matter. There the apples are still unrelated to the platter and without the identical contours of the later work.

60 STILL LIFE WITH BOTTLES, POTS, AND ALCOHOL STOVE, 1894-1900

Watercolor. 470 x 560. Venturi 1541. Mr. and Mrs. Leigh Block, Chicago.
Lionello Venturi, *Paul Cézanne Watercolours*, No. 17; Fritz Novotny, *Cézanne*, No. 114; Ctlg. *Paul Cézanne*, Art Institute of Chicago, Metropolitan Museum of Art, New York, 1952, No. 86 (repr.).
One type of still life of the later period uses bottles, jars, pots, and even an alcohol stove—objects which had in common their conical shapes—in a combination of oblong and circular forms. Cézanne used to develop such designs from simpler units (see V. 1148) to the most complex ones. The objects are tightly packed together without any air space to interfere. Like the skyscrapers in a modern city landscape, their cubic (or conical) forms create a rhythmical organization sideways, upwards, and into the third dimension. Never before in still lifes had so many ungainly objects been assembled into so crowded an area in so perfect a harmony. The colors are brown-yellow in the table and the bottles, blue and white in the metal utensils, a color combination as novel as the arrangement of the still life.

61 ORANGES ON A PLATTER, 1895-1900

Watercolor. 290 x 460. Venturi 1133. Wildenstein and Co. Mrs. Helen R. Tyson, Philadelphia.
Ctlg. *Cézanne,* Wildenstein and Co., New York, 1947, No. 80 (repr.).
There exists a nearly identical watercolor with a wine glass added (V. 1132). In the present watercolor, the white paper, rendering the table, contrasts vividly with the orange of the fruit, the blue-violet-green of the wallpaper, and the shadows of the fruit. The circulatory motion, the plasticity of the fruit, and the measurable distances of the verticals of the wallpaper create a simple and grand harmony that is expressive of our fundamental sensory experiences: space, direction, balance, and motion. Yet the flavor and the vibration of the real object is never lost.

62 HORTENSIAS, 1895-1900

Watercolor. 490 x 320. Venturi 1069. Wildenstein and Co. Siegfried Kramarsky, New York.
Ctlg. *Homage to Paul Cézanne,* Wildenstein & Co., London, 1939, No. 61; Ctlg. *Magic of Flowers in Painting,* Wildenstein and Co., New York, 1954, No. 9.
A large watercolor executed in a broad and simplified design. The red flower against the violet background is typical of the occasionally heated color

53

scheme of Cézanne's old age. The circular pot, the diagonal stems, the counter-diagonal of the curtain, crowned by the reddish ball of the hortensia, express a maximum of coherent and majestic design. However, the proportioned play of forms belongs at the same time to an atmospheric color-veil that subordinates the design under its fluent washes. It is the wholeness of the image that matters and not its individual parts.

63 THREE SKULLS, 1900-04

Watercolor. 480 x 630. Venturi 1131. Art Institute of Chicago.

Venturi has dedicated a special heading in his index of motifs to "Skulls." He enumerates twelve of them, and there are probably more. It seems meaningful that they appear only in his early and late years. The morbidity of youth and the melancholy of age lead him to a subject that is completely absent in the middle period of his life. Gasquet tells us that Cézanne liked to quote from a poem by Verlaine:

Le seul rire encore logique
Est celui des têtes de morts

and that he knew Baudelaire's *La Charogne* by heart (Joachim Gasquet, pp. 30-31). The skulls maintain their whiteness against the vivacious washes in green, red, and yellow of the large-patterned tablecloth. The empty sockets of noses and eyes are part of the haunting decorative pattern. Whereas in the early works the skulls show a character of rocklike solidity, they appear almost brittle in the late years. The artist varies the number of his skulls from one to three, achieving in this watercolor an architectural character.

LANDSCAPES

64 L'ESTAQUE, 1870-72

Pencil. 320 x 240. Not in Venturi. Verso of Pl. 13. Private collections, Berlin and New York. J. K. Thannhauser, New York.

Although the reverse of this drawing shows the likeness of little Paul, which would date it somewhere between 1878 and 1882, it seems to me more probable that Cézanne added the sketch of his son at a later time, since the style of this drawing closely recalls that of the winter landscape at L'Estaque (V. 51) executed in 1870-71.

The motive is skillfully chosen, although more picturesque than the artist later would have liked. All lines seem to come together in the left upper corner, while the roof of the house to the left connects with the piece of land in the foreground. The individual lines catch the appearance of the various objects but are not controlled—as in his drawings after 1882—by an even rhythm throughout. The tonal values are still somewhat accidental and do not relate to each other. What we enjoy then is the well-chosen view mingling the intimate with the distant and the fresh approach of the motive.

65 ENTRANCE INTO A GARDEN, 1872-77

Watercolor. 460 x 300. Venturi 842. W. Weinberg. Stephen Higgins, Paris. (Photo Hans Schreiner, Munich.)
Ctlg. *Cézanne Watercolors*, Fine Arts Associates, New York, 1956, No. 1 (repr.); Ctlg. *Paul Cézanne*, Den Haag, 1956, No. 54 (repr.); Ctlg. *Paul Cézanne*, Munich, 1956, No. 68 (repr.);

54

Ctlg. *Paul Cézanne*, Kunsthaus, Zurich, 1956, No. 91.

Probably done in Auvers, twenty miles from Paris, where Cézanne lived for a while with his wife in 1872, and where the scurrilous Dr. Gachet occasionally assembled the Impressionist painters at his house. Gachet owned several works by Cézanne which he left to the Louvre. Cézanne, attracted by the orderly and peaceful motive, drew the door a second time (V. 840). During his Impressionist epoch the artist sometimes yielded to his companions' predilections for the friendly and animated aspects of nature.

66 LANDSCAPE NEAR MELUN, c. 1877

Watercolor. 360 x 300. Venturi 972. Wildenstein and Co. Private collection, Europe.

Lionello Venturi, *Paul Cézanne Watercolours*, Fig. 3; Ctlg. *Cézanne*, Wildenstein and Co., New York, 1947, No. 69 (repr.); Georg Schmidt, *Watercolors by Paul Cézanne*, Fig. 7.

This is the most Impressionist watercolor in our selection. The date suggested by Georg Schmidt—1877—seems preferable to Venturi's dating, 1883-87. The artist is not at all interested in the structure of earth, trees, and houses and their interrelationship, but is totally absorbed by the vegetative carpet of the earth, its many-hued greens interrupted by the vivacious reds of the rooftops and a red field in the background. Here Cézanne comes closer to Renoir, Monet, and Pissarro than ever before. It is only in a certain wild loneliness that he differs in the character of his landscape. The rich variation of green tones, of yellowish meadows, and blue-green trees gives the opulence of summertime to the rural scene.

67 THE COTTAGE, c. 1880

Black chalk and watercolor. 310 x 475. Venturi 837 (dated 1872-77). The Home House Trustees, Courtauld Institute of Art, London.

Ctlg. *Cézanne Watercolors*, Tate Gallery, London, 1946, No. 3; Ctlg. *Landscape in French Art*, Royal Academy, London, 1949, No. 546; *The Home House Catalogue*, No. 23; *The Courtauld Collection*, 1954, No. 109 (repr.). The watercolor belongs to a group in which the artist explored the intimate aspects of a garden, such as a garden door (see Plate 65) or a wall. This idyllic touch, developed by the contact with the Impressionists, is rather unusual with Cézanne. The drawing emphasizes the horizontal of the garden wall with its built-in shack and extracts from it a mood of quiet order enlivened by a few diagonals. The washes, so evenly distributed over the surface, indicate that the watercolor does not belong in the early Impressionist period as Venturi dates it.

68 HOUSES IN PARIS (?), 1880-83

Pencil. 217 x 126. Not in Venturi. Mr. and Mrs. Leigh Block, Chicago.

John Rewald (ed.), *Paul Cézanne Carnet de Dessins*, Paris, 1951, I, 52, and II, 49 (repr.). From a sketch book owned by Mr. and Mrs. Block, p. vi.

No Impressionist painter would have chosen such a detail, with its unpicturesque parallelism of roof lines. To Cézanne, however, the natural geometry of the houses with their sober arrangement of horizontals and verticals had an immediate appeal. As in certain still lifes (see Plate 60), the drawing is not only proportioned sideways and upwards but is likewise developed in planes parallel with each other. Recession is brought about by a few diagonals. Compare with a similar view taken in L'Estaque, repr. *Paul Cézanne Sketch Book* (owned by the Art Institute of Chicago), New York, 1951, p. v, verso.

69 THE CASTLE OF MEDAN, 1879-81

Watercolor. 330 x 490. Venturi 847. Kunsthaus, Zurich.
Lionello Venturi, *Paul Cézanne Watercolours,* Fig. 19; Ctlg. *Paul Cézanne,* Den Haag, 1956, No. 57 (repr.); Ctlg. *Paul Cézanne,* Munich, 1956, No. 71 (repr.); Ctlg. *Paul Cézanne,* Kunsthaus, Zurich, 1956, No. 94, Fig. 49. Ctlg. Aix-en-Provence, 1956, No. 80.
Zola had acquired a house at the border of the Seine at Médan in 1878 and Cézanne became a frequent guest at his country place. The watercolor is nearly identical with the painting V. 325 in the museum in Glasgow that was once owned by Paul Gauguin. The position of the painter is on the opposite border of the Seine. From there quite naturally the horizontals of the border, of the road and hills, as contrasted with the verticals of houses and trees, present themselves and permitted the artist to base the organization of his watercolor on a pre-existent harmony in nature. The colors range from delicate greens over green-browns and green-blues to blue. Their values are still those of the Impressionist painters.

70 VIEW TOWARD THE MARSEILLE-VEYRE MOUNTAIN, 1882-85

Watercolor. 290 x 455. Venturi 915. Kunsthaus, Zurich.
Fritz Novotny, *Cézanne,* Pl. 94 (color);

Ctlg. *Paul Cézanne,* Kunsthaus, Zurich, 1956, No. 97; Ctlg. *Cézanne,* Aix-en-Provence, 1956, No. 68.
The scene represents another view of the Bay of Marseille and is identical with the painting V. 408. The red roofs of the houses form an evocative contrast with the blue-gray expansion of water and sky. Unlike the views of L'Estaque with their geometrical picture architecture, this painting expresses the atmospheric character of the motive. The absence of all unessential features, the generalized treatment of houses and trees, and the choice of the position so that the opposite coast of the bay appears above the roof line, lend the work its feeling of ordered vastness.

71 THE VILLAGE OF L'ESTAQUE, 1885-88

Black crayon. 290 x 460. Venturi 1503. Verso of V. 1047 (quarry). Dr. Gustav Radeke. Museum of Art, Rhode Island School of Design, Providence.
Bllt. Rhode Island School of Design, October, 1931, XIX, No. 4, p. 70; Bllt. Rhode Island School of Design, October, 1933, XXI, No. 4, pp. 49-52; Charles Slatkin and Regina Schoolman, *Six Centuries of French Master Drawings in America,* Pl. 110; Ctlg. *Paul Cézanne,* Art Institute of Chicago, Metropolitan Museum of Art, New York, 1952, Fig. 48.
This delicate drawing belongs to the large group of studies of the small industrial and harbor city of L'Estaque near Marseille, fifteen miles from Aix, where Cézanne lived at various times in his life. The Art Institute of Chicago (V. 493) and New York's Metropolitan Museum of Art (V. 429) own paintings of the same subject matter (Venturi enumerates thirty-eight of them). Cé-

zanne described them in a letter to Pissarro in 1876 as "like playing cards. Red roofs against the blue sea." It was the geometrical arrangement of the sober nineteenth-century houses with their many-sized cubes against the vast extension of the blue sea and the upper enclosure of the mountains which forever captivated the painter. He usually chooses a size of paper or canvas much wider than high, in order to emphasize the horizontal extension of the scene. In many of these sketches the white paper ground is left largely intact, in order to establish the façades of the houses, rendered by the white paper, as interrelated planes of equal value.

72 LANDSCAPE WITH BARE TREES, 1875-85

Pencil. 124 x 217. Not in Venturi. Art Institute of Chicago.
John Rewald (ed.), *Paul Cézanne Carnet de Dessins,* Paris, 1951, I, 35, and II, 55; Carl O. Schniewind (ed.), *Paul Cézanne Sketch Book* (owned by the Art Institute of Chicago), New York, 1951, I, 31, and II, xxxi.
The artist has here selected a view which permits him to arrange his picture space in parallel layers: trees with lawn, the river (?), the opposite border with houses. Solid forms are characterized by parallel lines of equal size and strength.

73 TREES AND SHRUBS, 1883-87

Pencil. 240 x 150. Venturi 1315. Adrien Chappuis, Tresserve (Savoie, France).
Adrien Chappuis, *Dessins de Paul Cézanne,* Paris, 1938, Pl. 31. From the third Chappuis sketch book, Pl. III verso.

The first denotation of a sunny corner in a garden, probably that of the "Jas de Bouffan," his parents' home. The silhouette of the tree in the foreground gives the feeling of organized space to the otherwise Impressionist rendering. The lesson of Pissarro can still be noticed in this drawing.

74 FOREST LANDSCAPE, c. 1885

Black pencil. 231 x 175. Verso: letter from 1885-86. Not in Venturi. Albertina, Vienna (inv. 24080).
Fritz Novotny, *Cézanne,* Pl. 120 (dated 1877-80).
The drawing seems related to such studies of trees as V. 419, in which the curved designs of stems or branches are explored, while in the later studies after 1885, the prismatic forms of straight lines and angles are emphasized.

75 TREES AND HOUSES, 1883-87

Pencil. 447 x 310. Not in Venturi. Alfred Flechtheim. Hans Purrmann, Montagnola.
Ctlg. *Paul Cézanne,* Den Haag, 1956, No. 120 (repr.); Ctlg. *Paul Cézanne,* Munich, 1956, No. 138 (repr.); Ctlg. *Paul Cézanne,* Kunsthaus, Zurich, 1956, No. 181, Fig. 71.
The drawing, undated in the previously mentioned exhibitions, represents probably the same scene as V. 1496, dated 1883-87. As in certain drawings by Corot, the supple vertical of trees creates mood and expression. The distance from tree to tree gives the experience of measured space. The roof of the cottage connects with the branch of the tree in the rear. The soft line of the path permits the eye to travel the entire depth of the picture.

76 TREES, 1885-87

Watercolor. 455 x 350. Venturi 980. Mrs. Grace R. Rogers. Mr. and Mrs. George Henry Warren, Newport.

The watercolor in its delicate feeling of growth develops the wavy and trembling rhythm of foliage and branches in a garden. It is as if the artist's geometric severity had relaxed for a short while to render the melodic similarity of the two trees. The prevailing tone is blue-violet contrasted with the brown in the stems and the wall in the background.

77 VALLEY OF THE ARC, 1883-87

Watercolor. 296 x 470. Venturi 913. Albertina, Vienna.

Ctlg. *Paul Cézanne,* Munich, 1956, No. 75 (repr.) ; Georg Schmidt, *Watercolors by Paul Cézanne,* Pl. 10; Fritz Novotny, *Cézanne,* Pl. 99.

Study for the paintings V. 452 and V. 453. See also Plate 78. Another rendering gives the view toward the viaduct, but shows only the lower branch of the tree as a framing motive (V. 454 and V. 455). The strongest color, green with blue, is in the crown of the tree. Only the first arches of the viaduct next to the tree are shaded in blue. The mountains behind are laid out in thin washes of blue, violet, and sienna. The application of the flat and overlying brush strokes comes closer to the technique of Turner and Constable than to that of the Impressionists. The middle ground links to the foreground at the meeting point of the branches of the pine tree with the viaduct. A photograph of the scene by John Rewald is reproduced in Fritz Novotny, *Cézanne und das Ende der Wissenschaftlichen Perspektive,* Vienna, 1938, Fig. 5. The use of a framing motive, traditional until the Impressionists discarded it, is rather unusual with Cézanne.

78 MONT SAINTE-VICTOIRE SEEN FROM A DISTANCE, 1885-87

Watercolor. 365 x 485. Venturi 1565. Hans Hahnloser, Bern. (Photo Hans Schreiner, Munich.)

Ctlg. *Paul Cézanne,* Munich, 1956, No. 77; Ctlg. *Paul Cézanne,* Kunsthaus, Zurich, 1956, No. 209.

See the remarks to the same subject in the Albertina drawing, Plate 77. This drawing is especially close to the drawing V. 1502. While in the Albertina drawing it is still the material aspect of tree, viaduct, and mountain that defines the character of the drawing, in this one the intangibles of space and distances within space create the picture. The essentials of the image are given sparcely and precisely. These essentials are the unity of color, which renders the enchantment of a sunlit world, and the extension of space measurable from distance to distance, which permits orientation within vastness. The importance of the undefined white paper as a true agent of the drawing recalls its use in Chinese scroll paintings.

79 PROVENCAL LANDSCAPE, 1885-87

Watercolor. 305 x 473. Not in Venturi. Mrs. A. Chester Beatty. Paul Rosenberg and Co., New York.

The scene is probably near the locality where Cézanne painted between 1885 and 1887, and which Venturi entitles *Pin et Terres Rouges* (V. 458 and V. 459). This drawing, seemingly never before published, is unusual in Cézanne's later work by the prevalence of curved lines over the usual horizontal-vertical organization. As in his view toward the aqueduct and Mont Sainte-Victoire (V. 914), the artist uses a tree with branches extended over the entire width of the paper to give his motive a foreground enclosure. Yet in conformity with the dominant form of the drawing the tree is not straight and parallel with the paper edge but is diagonal. The feeling of wind-blown trees and sweeping hills is suggested.

80 THE TREES IN X FORM, 1888-97

Watercolor. 405 x 555. Venturi 938. Private collection, Switzerland. (Photo H. Wullschleger, Winterthur.)
Fritz Novotny, *Paul Cézanne*, No. 108. In this large watercolor, the curious effect of two crossing trees attracted the artist. Another version of the theme is known (V. 937). The geometrical pattern is further enhanced by touches of green, blue, and yellow which follow a horizontal-vertical arrangement. The lines are drawn with a fine and pointed brush—nearly penlike in effect—contrasting in their precise definition with the broad atmospheric color veil. Notice how the branches to the left are adjusted to each other in their curvilinear shapes. The controlled agitation of the rendering gives an effect of majesty.

81 STUDY OF A TREE, c. 1895

Pencil. 300 x 460. Not in Venturi. Mrs. Langton Douglas. Mr. and Mrs. Perry T. Rathbone, Cambridge, Massachusetts.
Centenaire du Peintre Indépendant Paul Cézanne, Orangerie, Paris, 1939,

No. 51; John Rewald, *Paul Cézanne*, New York, 1948, Fig. 98; *St. Louis Collections*, City Art Museum, St. Louis, 1948, No. 61; *Nineteenth Century French Drawings*, California Palace of the Legion of Honor, San Francisco, 1947, No. 3; Ctlg. *Cézanne*, Fine Arts Associates, New York, 1952, No. 8 (repr.).
Again and again Cézanne felt compelled to draw trees. Irregular growth, as much as the column-like geometry of the trunks, fascinated his eyes. Here, as in many of the sketch-book drawings, the forms are delicately put down, as if the artist were afraid to intrude with a temperamental stroke into the silent existence of the world of objects. The shape of the trunk and the long branch parallel the shape of the paper.

82 HOUSE IN PROVENCE, 1890-94

Watercolor. 420 x 535. Venturi 958. Bernheim-Jeune. J. K. Thannhauser. Henry Pearlman, New York.
Ctlg. *Paul Cézanne*, Art Institute of Chicago, Metropolitan Museum of Art, New York, 1952, No. 102 (repr.); Ctlg. *Cézanne*, Aix-en-Provence, 1956, No. 73. Ctlg. *Cézanne Watercolors*, Fine Arts Associates, New York, 1956, No. 12 (repr.).
The soft richness of the blue, violet, and green color spots lends to the scene a nearly magic quality, enhanced by the large size of the paper and the symmetrical frontality. The drawing emanates the silent peace of a summer day.

83 LANDSCAPE WITH TREES, 1890-94

Watercolor. 290 x 460. Not in Venturi. P. J. Bachman. Walter Arensberg.

Philadelphia Museum of Art, Louise and Walter Arensberg Collection.

Ctlg. *European Master Drawings of the 19th and 20th Centuries*, Mills College Art Gallery, Oakland, 1939, No. 14 (repr.); Ctlg., Art Institute of Chicago, 1949, No. 37 (repr.); *Arensberg Collection*, Philadelphia Museum of Art, 1954, No. 32 (repr.).

Cézanne is here not so much interested in the graphic expressiveness of the tree trunks as in the color tapestry of the foliage. As in many paintings of the same period, he applies the color in diagonally parallel strokes which lend a uniform "weave" to the equally textured surface.

84 PISTACHIO TREE AT CHATEAU NOIR, 1895-1900

Watercolor. 535 x 431. Venturi 1040. Art Institute of Chicago.

Ctlg. *Paul Cézanne*, Art Institute of Chicago, Metropolitan Museum of Art, New York, 1952, No. 99 (repr.); Ctlg. *Paul Cézanne*, Den Haag, 1956, No. 76 (repr.); Ctlg. *Paul Cézanne*, Munich, 1956, No. 95 (repr.); Ctlg. *Paul Cézanne*, Kunsthaus, Zurich, 1956, No. 123, Fig. 56.

The reddish-violet tones which predominate in the late work of the artist prevail also in this watercolor. The calligraphy of the branches stands out against a blue sky. The large size of the drawing enhances its monumental character. One notices how the bulbous form of the tree trunk is carried over into some of the air-space between the branches. A rhythmical continuity organizes even the most twisted and irregular forms of the tree. A precarious balance between wild growth and order is established.

85 THE BALCONY, 1890-1900

Watercolor. 550 x 390. Venturi 1126. Philadelphia Museum of Art, A. E. Gallatin Collection.

Ctlg. *Paul Cézanne*, Art Institute of Chicago, Metropolitan Museum of Art, New York, 1952, No. 124; *A. E. Gallatin Collection*, Philadelphia Museum of Art, 1954, No. 28 (repr. p. 11).

As in the drawings *Coat Over a Chair* (Plate 57) and *Unmade Bed* (Plate 51), a close-up enlarges the object—the rail—beyond our normal view. The forms of the grill of the balcony loom big and nearly threatening. They are conceived by the painter as a wheel-like motion which stirs the colors of the background into vibrancy.

86 ROCKY RIDGE, 1895-1900

Watercolor. 315 x 470. Venturi 1043. Museum of Modern Art, New York, Lillie P. Bliss Collection.

Göran Schildt, *Paul Cézannes Personlighet, etc.*, Fig. 57; Fritz Novotny, *Cézanne*, Pl. 107; Ctlg. *Paul Cézanne*, Art Institute of Chicago, Metropolitan Museum of Art, New York, 1952, No. 106 (repr.).

During his last years, Cézanne drove out to the stone quarry of Bibémus where he studied the geological architecture of nature, modified and enhanced by the irregular plant life and the play of sunlight and shadows over the surfaces. A grand terrestrial spectacle with cyclopic blocks and slanting trees unfolded before the eyes of the painter, so utterly different from what he had seen and noticed in younger years. V. 1042-1060 deal with this and adjacent motifs. Plate 87 shows another version of this site. As in the drawing *Unmade Bed* (Plate 51), the artist is stirred by the interplay of geometrical patterns with bulbous and cloudlike formations. A few trees in the center and to the right offer a skeleton-design of basic directions.

87 ROCKS AT BIBEMUS, 1895-1900

Watercolor. 470 x 305. Venturi 1044. Ward Cheney. Joseph Pulitzer, Jr., St Louis.
Ctlg. *Cézanne*, Fine Arts Associates, New York, 1952, No. 9; Ctlg. *Cézanne Watercolors*, Fine Arts Associates, New York, 1956, No. 17; Ctlg. *Louise and Joseph Pulitzer Collection*, New York and Cambridge, 1957, No. 16, Fig. 8.
See the remarks to Plate 86, dealing with the same subject matter. Here the washes are in rust, blue, and green. Instead of the horizontal development of the rock stratifications, the view this time emphasizes the vertical structure. A branch reaches from above toward the cyclopic walls. Its undulating organic form contrasts with the prismatic shapes of the rock. One thinks of Cézanne's statement to Gasquet: "I wanted to make from Impressionism something as solid and durable as the art of the museums" (Joachim Gasquet, *Cézanne*, p. 148).

88 CHATEAU NOIR, 1895-1900

Pencil with touches of watercolor. 360 x 526. Venturi 1034. Museum Boymans, Rotterdam. (Photo A. Frequin, Den Haag.)
After his paternal estate, the beloved "Jas de Bouffan," had to be sold in 1899, Cézanne was in search of new motives. He returned to his cabin near the Bibémus quarry and rented a small room in the Château Noir, halfway between Aix and Le Tholonet. He felt so attracted by the wild and rocky scenery from which the house with its Gothic windows rose (see the photograph of the locality in John Rewald, *Paul Cézanne*, New York, 1948, Fig. 109) that he offered to buy the property, but the owner did not want to sell.
Venturi reproduces four watercolors of the subject matter (V. 1025, V. 1034-1036). In this drawing the straight and quiet pencil lines prevail over the violet, blue, and green of the foliage. In the other watercolors, especially in V. 1036, the reddish-tinted building seems nearly submerged by the onrush of the straggling vegetation. The same dramatic exaltation animates the oil paintings of the same scene (V. 667, V. 765, V. 794-797). In contrast, this drawing is a study of delicate restraint and crystalline clarity.

89 THE TURN OF THE PATH, 1895-1904

Watercolor. 301 x 470. Venturi 1071. Mrs. A. Chester Beatty. Paul Rosenberg and Co., New York.
Typical for the late oils and watercolors is the disappearance of the network of lines and the dissolution of solid forms into a veil of blue-violet colors. The world becomes less tangible and more immaterial but also less static and more vehement. The slanting touches of the brush move with great speed from the upper right toward the lower left. This dynamic flow is related to the expressive curve of the road, indicated merely by the white paper. This intensification of color and form inspired the Fauve painters Matisse, Derain, Dufy, and Vlaminck of the succeeding generation (see the oil by Derain, Plate D).

61

90 WALL WITH TREES, 1890-1900

Watercolor. 310 x 470. Venturi 1066.
Erich Maria Remarque, Ascona.
Ctlg. *Paul Cézanne,* Den Haag, 1956,
No. 72 (repr.) ; Ctlg. *Paul Cézanne,*
Munich, 1956, No. 87 (repr.) ; Ctlg.
Paul Cézanne, Kunsthaus, Zurich, 1956,
No. 112.
Matter, space, and light create here a
poetic evocation on the borderline be-
tween representation and abstraction.
Touches of yellow, green, and violet
adhere to the surface. And yet, in spite
of the delicacy of the colors, the struc-
ture of lines, the measured recession in
space makes the watercolor solid beyond the possibility of change.

91 TREES AT THE WATER, c. 1900

Watercolor. 320 x 490. Venturi 1552.
Erich Maria Remarque, Ascona.
Ctlg. *Paul Cézanne,* Den Haag, 1956,
No. 80 (repr.) ; Ctlg. *Paul Cézanne,*
Munich, 1956, No. 103 (repr.) ; Ctlg.
Paul Cézanne, Kunsthaus, Zurich, 1956,
No. 131, Fig. 60.
The magic of this watercolor rests on
its supreme balance between the tangible line work of the leafless trees and
the ethereal vapor of violet and green
color touches not related to any defined
form. In the lower section, these touches
indicate the horizontal-vertical orientation of the painting ground (= poten-
tial space) ; in the upper section, they
turn diagonally and create the at-
mospheric-coloristic echo of the diagonals of the trees. Besides, by the
gradation of the color intensity, they
indicate distance from the spectator
and weight of matter. Line and color
are not isolated, but each is the carrier
of a multiplicity of aesthetic functions.

The result is an ordered universe, de-
prived of its material particularizations.

92 MONT SAINTE-VICTOIRE, c. 1902

Watercolor. 305 x 482. Not in Venturi.
Ambroise Vollard. Reid and Lefevre
Ltd. Bignou Gallery. Sam Salz. Mr. and
Mrs. Paul Hirschland, New York.
(Photo Colten, New York.)
Ctlg. *Watercolors by Cézanne,* Reid and
Lefevre Ltd., London, 1937, No. 12;
Ctlg. *Paintings by French Masters—
Delacroix to Dufy,* Montreal, 1938, No.
5; Ctlg. *Paintings and Watercolors by
Cézanne,* Bignou Gallery, New York,
1940, No. 16; Lionello Venturi, *Paul
Cézanne Watercolours,* Pl. 21; Ctlg.
Nineteenth Century French Drawings,
California Palace of the Legion of
Honor, San Francisco, 1947, No. 114;
Ctlg. *Watercolors of an Earlier Day,*
Fine Arts Gallery, San Diego, 1951, No.
18; Ctlg. *Cézanne,* Fine Arts Associates,
New York, 1953, No. 15 (repr.).
This watercolor is probably related to
V. 665 and V. 666, dated by Venturi
1894-1900. A photograph of the actual
site, taken by John Rewald, is reproduced in Fritz Novotny, *Cézanne,*
Fig. 12. The Sainte-Victoire Mountain
is really a mountain ridge of rugged
limestone that dominates the Valley of
the Arc and the city of Aix. However,
from the position chosen by the painter,
the massif presents itself foreshortened
in the shape of a single mountain. It appears here in great and simple forms,
not seen from a great distance as usual,
but close, large, and threatening, executed with predominantly blue washes.
Only the formation of the hills and
mountains is rendered; vegetation and
houses are omitted. A geological drama
is created by the barrenness of the

scene and the dynamic stretching of the lines.

93 VALLEY OF THE ARC, 1902-06

Watercolor. 240 x 301. Not in Venturi. Ambroise Vollard. Ruscher. Frank. Wildenstein and Co. Private collection, United States.

This watercolor represents the last and most abstract phase in the work of the artist. The view over the wide valley of Aix with the viaduct in the distance (see Plates 77 and 78) has yielded to a reorganization of the visible data into a new configuration. With delicate touch the brush establishes the color weave of the foliage and atmosphere, while horizontal and vertical lines, drawn with the brush, create distance and direction. Immaterial yet thoroughly organized, half-abstract yet atmospheric, Cézanne now evolves an art "parallel to nature" rather than referring to nature.

PLATES

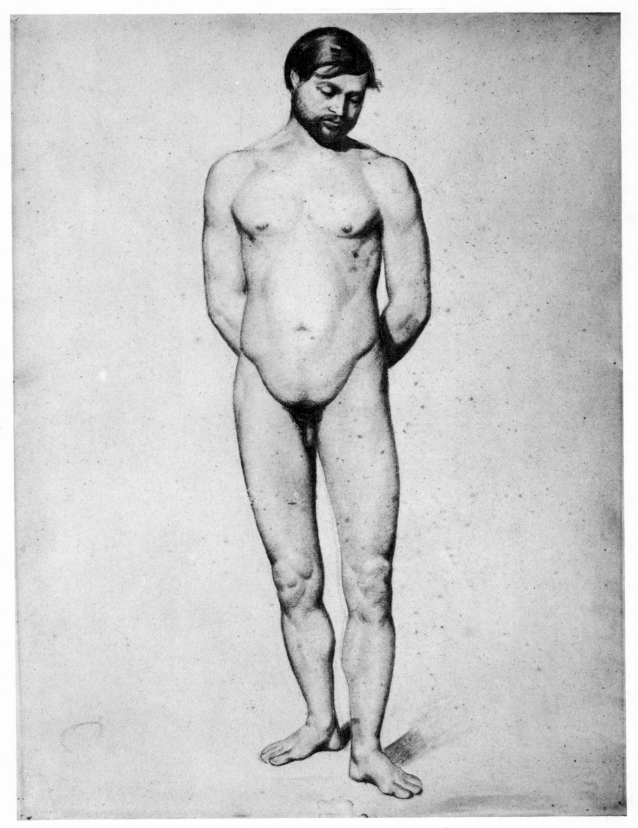

1 MALE NUDE   1862

2 NUDE MALE FIGURE SEEN FROM THE BACK

1859-62

3 ROWING MEN   1865-70

4 STUDY FOR "THE AUTOPSY"   1865-67

5 STUDY FOR "L'APRÈS-MIDI A NAPLES"   1872-73

6 MAN SURROUNDED BY RATS   1875

7 TWO WOMEN AT THE EDGE OF A RIVER 1872-77

8 OLYMPIA   1875-77

9 WOMAN BATHER   1873-82

10 STUDY AFTER RUBENS' "LANDING OF   c. 1880
    MARIE DE MEDICI IN MARSEILLE"

11 BATHERS REPOSING

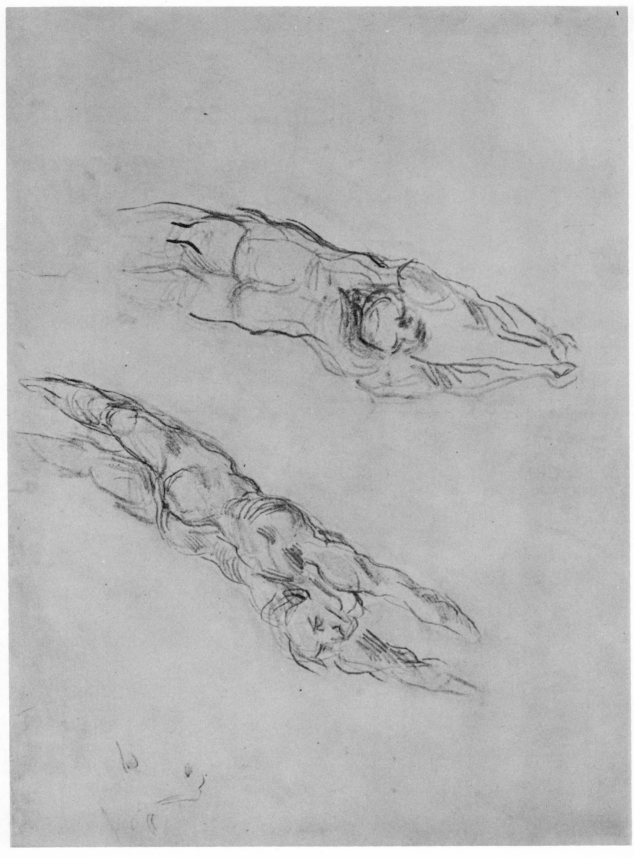

13 SKETCHES AROUND A BAROQUE ENGRAVING   1878

1879-82

16 THE BATHER

1878-82

15 THE BATHER

1879-82  18 MEDEA AFTER DELACROIX

1879-85 17 THE ENTOMBMENT AFTER CARAVAGGIO

19 AMOR AFTER PUGET'S STATUE IN THE LOUVRE   1888-95

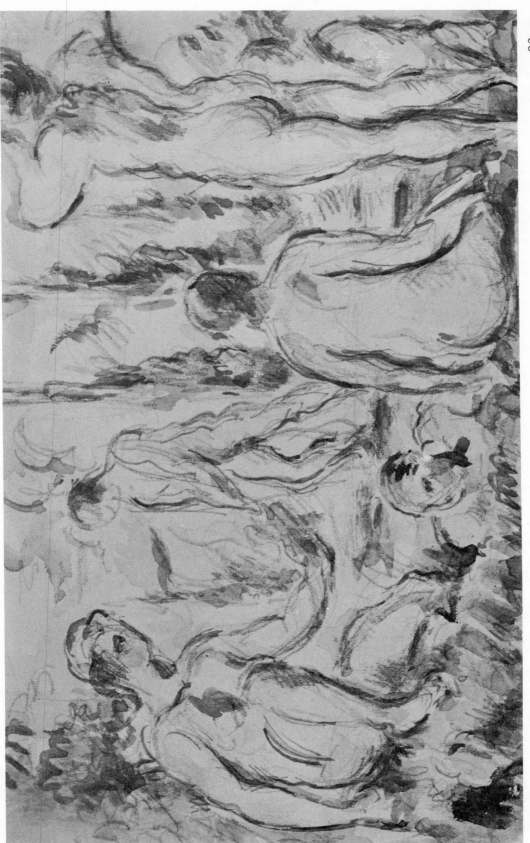

20 BATHERS

21 NUDE AFTER SIGNORELLI   1882-90

22 ST. GEORGE AFTER DONATELLO

1885-95

23 HARLEQUIN   1888

24 STUDY OF A NUDE FIGURE

1885-95

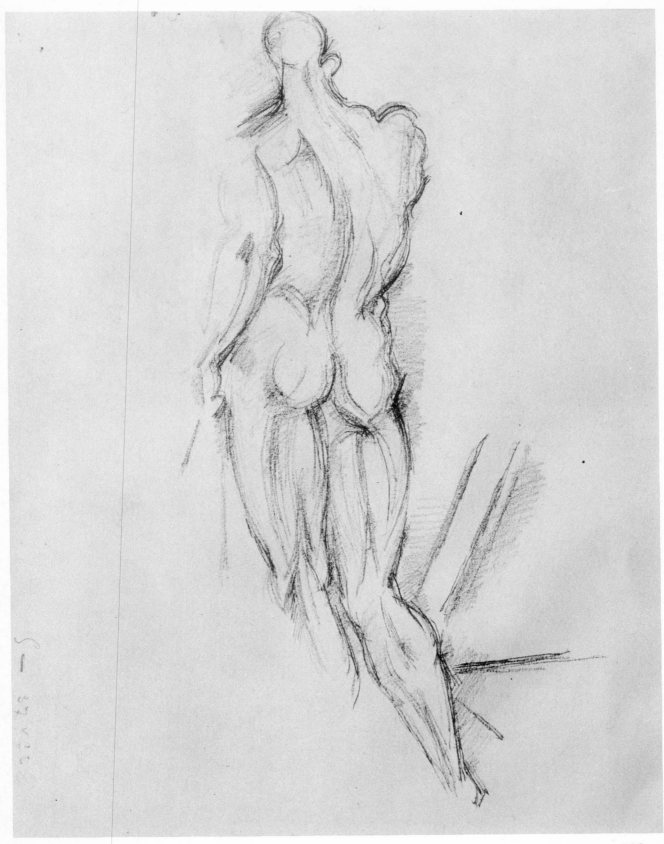

25 STUDY AFTER HOUDON'S "L'ECORCHÉ"   1888-95

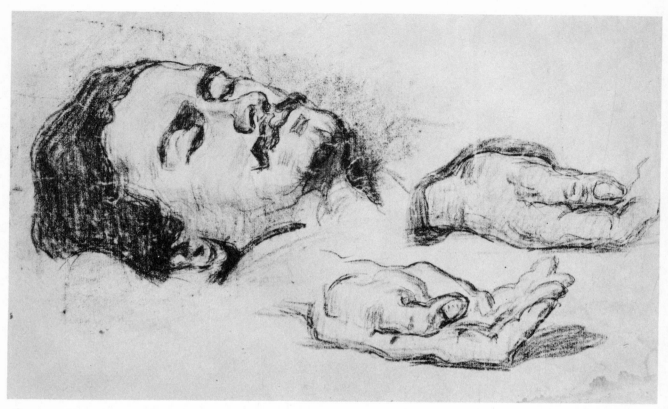

26 HEAD AND HAND STUDIES OF THE PAINTER   1867-69
   ACHILLE EMPERAIRE

27 CÉZANNE'S FATHER READING A NEWSPAPER   1868-70

28 PORTRAIT OF CAMILLE PISSARRO   C. 1873

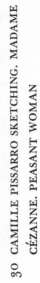

30 CAMILLE PISSARRO SKETCHING. MADAME
CÉZANNE. PEASANT WOMAN   C. 1881

1872-76

29 PORTRAIT OF PISSARRO

31 SELF PORTRAIT   1875-77

32 SELF PORTRAIT   1880-82

XXXVII

33 SELF PORTRAIT   1885-86

34 SELF PORTRAIT   c. 1895

35 PORTRAIT OF MADAME CÉZANNE   1880-85

36 MADAME CÉZANNE   c. 1890

37 MADAME CÉZANNE   1883-86

39 THE ARTIST'S SON PAUL   1880-82

38 PORTRAIT OF THE ARTIST'S SON   1880-82

40 THE FATHER OF THE ARTIST   1880-86

41 STUDY FOR THE HARLEQUIN IN "MARDI GRAS" 1888

42 PORTRAIT OF A PEASANT   1890-92

43 THE CARD PLAYER   1890-92

44 HEAD OF RICHELIEU   1890-95

45 BOY WITH THE RED VEST   1890-95

46 PORTRAIT OF VOLLARD 1899

47 SEATED PEASANT   1900-04

48 THE GARDENER VALLIER   1900-06

49 THE GREEN JAR

1885-95

50 CANDLE HOLDER AND DIVERSE OBJECTS   1894-1900

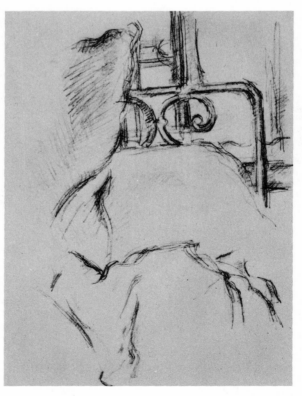

51 UNMADE BED   after 1880

52 ROCOCO CLOCK   after 1885

53 ORNAMENT IN THE STYLE OF LOUIS XIV
after 1885

54 THREE PEARS   1888

55 STILL LIFE WITH EGGPLANT, POMEGRANATES, 1895-1905
   A SUGAR BOWL, AND A CARAFE ON A TABLE

56 STILL LIFE WITH SOUP BOWL AND BRONZE GOBLET c. 1890

57 COAT OVER A CHAIR   1890-1900

58 APPLES AND INK BOTTLE   1895-1900

59 SIX APPLES   1895-1900

60 STILL LIFE WITH BOTTLES, POTS, AND   1894-1900
    ALCOHOL STOVE

61 ORANGES ON A PLATTER   1895-1900

63 THREE SKULLS   1900-04

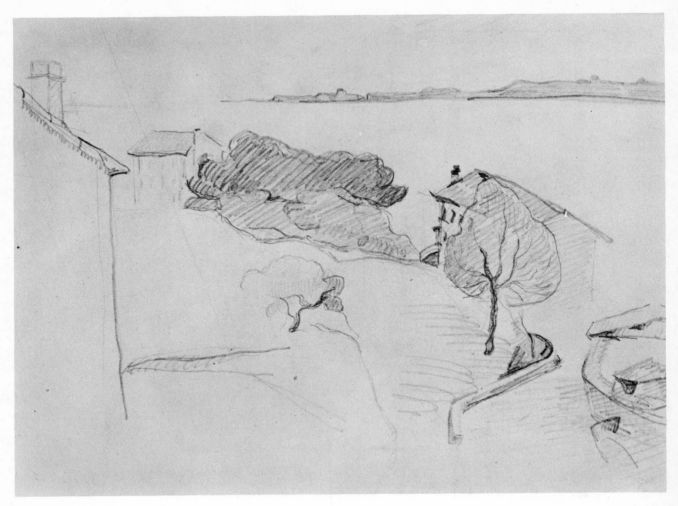

64 L'ESTAQUE

1870-72

65 ENTRANCE INTO A GARDEN   1872-77

66 LANDSCAPE NEAR MÉLUN · C. 1877

67 THE COTTAGE   C. 1880

68 HOUSES IN PARIS (?)   1880-83

69 THE CASTLE OF MÉDAN 1879-81

70 VIEW TOWARD THE MARSEILLEVEYRE MOUNTAIN   1882-85

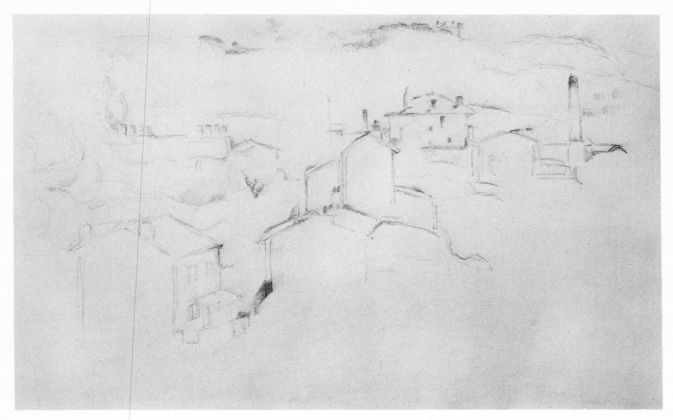

71 THE VILLAGE OF L'ESTAQUE   1885-88

72 LANDSCAPE WITH BARE TREES   1875-85

73 TREES AND SHRUBS   1883-87

74 FOREST LANDSCAPE   C. 1885

75 TREES AND HOUSES

1883-87

76 TREES   1885-87

77 VALLEY OF THE ARC   1883-87

78 MONT SAINTE-VICTOIRE SEEN FROM A DISTANCE   1885-87

79 PROVENCAL LANDSCAPE   1885-87

80 THE TREES IN X FORM   1888-97

81 STUDY OF A TREE   c. 1895

82 HOUSE IN PROVENCE   1890-94

83 LANDSCAPE WITH TREES   1890-94

84 PISTACHIO TREE AT CHATEAU NOIR   1895-1900

85 THE BALCONY   1890-1900

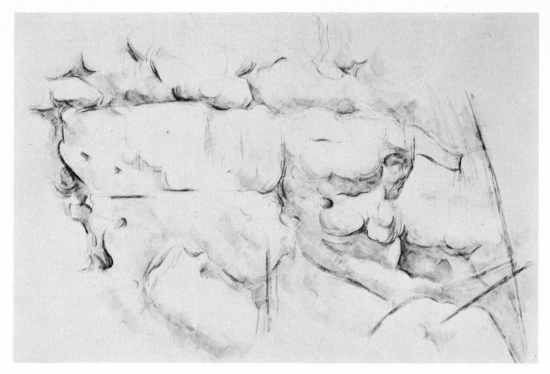

86 ROCKY RIDGE 1895-1900

87 ROCKS AT BIBÉMUS 1895-1900

88 CHATEAU NOIR   1895-1900

89 THE TURN OF THE PATH   1895-1904

90 WALL WITH TREES

1890-1900

91 TREES AT THE WATER   C. 1900

92 MONT SAINTE-VICTOIRE   C. 1902

93 VALLEY OF THE ARC   1902-06

A EUGENE DELACROIX. STUDY FOR THE APOLLO CEILING IN
THE LOUVRE. OIL. JAQUES SELIGMAN AND CO., NEW YORK.

B HANS VON MARÉES. NUDE. PENCIL. WUPPERTAL-ELBERFELD,
STAEDTISCHES MUSEUM.

C PABLO PICASSO. LANDSCAPE. OIL. JOSEPH
PULITZER, ST. LOUIS, MISSOURI, U. S. A.

D ANDRÉ DERAIN. LANDSCAPE. OIL. SEATTLE MUSEUM OF ART,
WASHINGTON, U. S. A.